NOT IN MY PHILOSOPHY:

True experiences of the
supernatural and the search
for explanations

Not in my philosophy:
True experiences of the supernatural and the search for explanations

Published by The Conrad Press in the United Kingdom 2021

Tel: +44(0)1227 472 874
www.theconradpress.com
info@theconradpress.com

ISBN 978-1-914913-10-5

Typesetting and Cover Design by: Charlotte Mouncey, www.bookstyle.co.uk
The Conrad Press logo was designed by Maria Priestley.

Printed and bound in Great Britain by Clays Ltd, Elcograf S.p.A.

NOT IN MY PHILOSOPHY

True experiences of the
supernatural and the search
for explanations

PATRICIA MARSH

Contents

PROLOGUE

I am an atheist and an academic. My life has been ruled by the search for knowledge, a love of research and intellectual discussion. I have come to the conclusion that human beings are just a collection of chemicals and energy, like all life forms – no 'soul' of any kind, nothing unique to each of us – and I have been happy and contented. I've come to see that living on after death is true in a genetic sense: my children have inherited my genes as I have those of my own parents. I become more and more aware as the years go by of how much of what I do is determined by those genes, even down to little tics and the way I draw in my lips.

But I have kept a guilty secret for fifty years. The circles in which I have moved – mainly highly educated people, some of them university lecturers and professors – all hold it to be a fact of life that there is nothing supernatural, that science has basically answered all the questions that needed to be answered, and that anything supposedly paranormal must be bogus, explicable either as some kind of sensory illusion, or as an out-and-out fake. Hence, I have imbibed the message from early on in my career that revealing my guilty secret would mark me out as an embarrassment and ultimately lead to rejection by my peer group, the worst of all fates for someone like me, who is rather gregarious and needs approval.

But retirement brings with it a reckoning with self. No matter how busy you become with all kinds of projects and good works, the lack of everyday contact with like-minded colleagues means you are left to think things through on your own much of the time. So now I have to face the anomalies in my life, the events which I myself, or those close to me, have experienced and which are not dreamt of in my philosophy. It's time to stop posing and face head-on the apparition, premonitions, pain telepathy, prophetic dream, poltergeists, inception, clairvoyance, palmistry, stunning coincidences and – worst of all – being in two places at once. I have to be honest and recognise that these are at odds with my philosophy of life.

This book is an account of these strange experiences. None of this is fiction, except for a few names and descriptive details which I can't remember, but which have no bearing on the truth of the incident. I wrote down what happened at the time, so there are no false memories here.

At the end of each account, I'll look into explanations which have been given for the strange events I describe. I'll hope to find something to guide me in changing my philosophy of life and perhaps give you, the reader, some insights. I'm going to overcome my prejudices and seek the views of experts in all fields of the supernatural, whether they be respected physicists, world-renowned biologists, parapsychologists, paraphysicists, philosophers, people of religion, or established mediums and clairvoyants with a proven record.

My experiences have provided a glimpse into something much greater and more profound than our everyday reality, and I'm determined to open the door a little wider into that world.

1.

The ginger kitten: 1969

Anima, souls, daemons and bioplasma

What is it that, when present in a body, makes it living?
— A soul.

SOCRATES

The persistence of some questionable phenomena that science ignores,
such as the possibility of an afterlife as well as certain paranormal
phenomena, continually cause problems for science precisely because
science ignores them when in fact they will not go away.

JAMES BEICHLER, *TO DIE FOR*

I must have been skilled at crying in a way that draws sympathy and compliance when I was two years old. I calculate I must have been that age when our kitten was killed in a road accident. It can't have been more than a few months old and must have been pretty unlucky – cars were not so common on Highway Road, Leicester, in 1952.

In spite of the fact that my elder brother Richard, five at the time, had been promised a dog when this kitten died and that my mother clearly loved dogs – she had a large set of dark green encyclopaedias about them – my inconsolable weeping about the untimely death of the kitten won the day, and we got another kitten as our family pet. My brother had to resign himself to another cat, but was careful to extract a cast-iron commitment from my parents that, when this cat expired, even if it happened the day after tomorrow, we would buy a dog.

The new kitten was ginger and male. We called him Sandy. He grew into a huge cat and, even though he'd been neutered, he was a street fighter, regularly appearing in the morning with a scratched face or hole in his fur. After one of these nocturnal encounters, he had a torn and ragged left ear for life. My father and brother took to calling him Ginger Bum, his impressive hindquarters being his most salient feature.

In the nature of cats, Sandy was standoffish and supercilious, very particular about his food and requiring cream rather than milk to drink. (In the 1950s and, in fact, for all of Sandy's life, we were unaware that most cats are lactose intolerant – Sandy certainly seemed blissfully ignorant of this fact, which all cat owners today will inform you about in no uncertain terms.) He did know, however, that my mother was soft-hearted and an animal lover, so he trained her well in his alimentary likes and dislikes.

In return, Sandy performed an excellent job as a mouser and would regularly leave the remains of his nocturnal rodent control on the back doorstep. He became the object of great admiration one day when my mother opened the back door to discover a large dead rat. Sandy bore the scars of an epic battle with this creature, but his satisfaction at hearing us all exclaim admiringly about his great feat was evident in his loud purring. Our cat had the laryngeal muscles and vocal cords of a feline Pavarotti; his purr could compete with a tractor and certainly drown out a BBC announcer on the Home Service.

Sadly, though, our ginger tom must have been unaware of Mum's membership of the Royal Society for the Protection of

Birds. She didn't show the expected delight at having a starling as the back-doorstep offering one morning. Sandy tried a variety of other species of bird as gifts without success, and was clearly indignant at the lack of thanks my mother expressed. He would deprive us of his presence for a few hours as a result, and often disappeared from view completely until the next mealtime.

This was the case one day when Richard was experimenting in the shed at the bottom of the garden with the chemistry set my parents had – unwisely, in my opinion – bought him for his birthday. He managed to create a stupendous explosion; the number of decibels must have been over a hundred. It didn't blow the roof off the shed or anything – it just made a very loud bang. Anyway, it was extremely effective in flushing Sandy out of his hiding-place in the garden – which must have been somewhere around the shed. All I saw was a ginger streak flashing at lightning speed from the compost heap at the bottom of our long garden to the lilac tree outside the French windows. It finally reconstituted itself into a large cat quivering among the perennials.

Now I'm not accusing my brother of carrying out this experiment with the sole purpose of hastening our cat's end, but he may well have reflected afterwards that this might soon result.

I myself was responsible for another incident which could well have shortened poor Sandy's existence. He would sometimes allow me to pick him up and place him on my lap to be stroked with one hand while I read the next chapter of my textbook for homework, inevitably accompanied by the seismic vibrations and volume of his voice production.

On one memorable occasion, I was alone in the house and had sunk into a reverie from the combination of the rhythmic purring on my lap and the somewhat stultifying text concerning tea plantations in India I was reading. A travelling salesman chose that moment to ring our front door bell. The high-pitched chime startled me out of my stupor and I leapt up, projecting cat and geography textbook across the room to quite a distance. Sandy understandably found it hard to forgive and forget this sudden assault on his nerves and dignity. Never again did he relax so completely on my lap or purr quite so loudly, and indeed he permitted himself to be placed there much less frequently.

In spite of this, there was a bond between us; perhaps Sandy somehow knew he owed his existence to me insisting on having another kitten when I was two. He may even have had siblings which had been drowned because they had found no one to take them in. This was common practice at the time.

Throughout my childhood and teenage years, it was always to Sandy I turned in moments of joy or despair. If I miraculously passed a maths exam, I would bury my face in his fur and whoop with triumph; if a boy I fancied ignored me, I would weep into his lush ginger coat inconsolably. Sandy was remarkably forbearing on these occasions.

My brother went off to boarding school at the age of thirteen and Sandy was there to greet him on his reappearance at the end of each term. Indeed, he was still pet-in-residence when Richard went off to university. Sandy was himself thirteen years old by then – Mum informed us that was ninety-one in cat years.

Three years later and Sandy was still there to wave a sad paw – metaphorically speaking, though he clearly had some anthropomorphic features – as I departed for Paris to spend an unexpectedly exciting six months as an au pair in 1968. Yes, I was to be there in the thick of the famous May student revolution.

I remember one of Mum's weekly letters during this period included a frightening account of Sandy's coughing and spluttering one day, leading my parents to think he was about to expire. In the end, he simply brought up a particularly large furball and then stretched out in front of the fire again. When I came home from Paris, tricolore in hand, he seemed a little slower in his movements and yet more obese than I remembered, but he continued to be the main hearth installation in the dining room.

The following month I set off to study French for three years at the University of Bristol. I had a room in Manor Hall in Clifton, that most beautiful of English city suburbs. The Hall asked me to move out for my second year and be a house warden for one of the student houses in the Georgian terrace opposite the main building. I vaguely remember some kind of duties about locking the door at 11pm and making sure no one had a man in their room after dark – not that I remember checking.

The culmination of this story is about me coming down to lock the front door one night in that second year at university. I think that's what I was doing. My room was on the top floor at the back, so I don't think I could have heard the kitten mewing from up there and come down to investigate. No, for some reason I was at the front door late one night and heard the most pathetic mews coming from outside. Being a cat owner and lover at the time, I could hardly ignore such evidence of feline distress, so I was quick to open the door. There on the mat was a ginger kitten looking up at me, its eyes ineffably appealing. It got swept up into my arms and taken upstairs, where a saucer of milk was laid before it. It lapped the milk up with its rough little tongue and went on mewing until I picked it up again and stroked it gently. Its purr was no match for Sandy's, but was pretty loud for a kitten, I must say.

The woollen rug Mum had given me to take to uni in case I got cold on those Bristol nights was pulled out of the built-in cupboard in the corner of my large room, and a drawer was unceremoniously emptied of underwear and pressed into service as a makeshift bed for the orphan who had come to my door. Had it escaped from the drowner's sack? How had it found its way to me? The ginger kitten was laid, still purring, on the rug in the drawer and I readied myself for bed. The fact that I had a basin in my room for washing my face and brushing my teeth meant I could keep an eye on my little visitor while I carried out my night-time ablutions.

'Nigh-night,' I said to the ginger kitten, which looked as if it was on its way to the Land of Nod by then, having waggled its ears backwards and forwards quite vigorously while contemplating my strange activities at the basin.

I lay awake for some time wondering what I would do with him (Mum had told me that all ginger cats are male, so I also got sidetracked into wondering about the genetic processes which produced a ginger tom from a non-ginger female). This must have lulled me to sleep because the next thing I remember was waking up in the morning with the sun already quite high in the sky. I shot out of bed, eager to see my new ginger kitten. His bed was empty so I searched all round the room to find him, making that kind of kissing noise used to call cats, but it was all in vain. He was nowhere to be found. My door was closed. In horror, I forced myself to look out the slightly open high sash window in case the kitten had climbed up the curtain and ejected itself through the minute gap at the top, though that would hardly have been feasible. There was no ginger splat on the lawn outside. I opened my door and went down the stairs, calling as I went. I opened the front door and looked about – nothing.

I was in the hall when the phone started ringing. We had one phone for the eight women in the house – that was the norm in those primitive times. Whoever was nearest would answer it and then fetch whoever the caller required. In this case, there was no need to do that. It was Mum. She rarely called me – we were still on our weekly letter regime.

'I'm afraid I have bad news, dear. It's Sandy. He's not been himself for the past few days and, late last night, I'm sorry to tell you, he died. It was all quite peaceful in the end, though. I know you'll be very upset but he really did have a good innings, didn't he? Seventeen years old – that's a hundred and nineteen in cat years. We never imagined he'd last so long, poor old thing. Well, I thought you should know. I know how you loved him – dear Sandy. Too late for Richard to have his dog now . . .'

This was all very distressing and I momentarily forgot about my ginger kitten guest while the news sank in. When I'd put the phone down, I remembered. I searched the whole house, the street and the gardens.

I never did find that kitten.

෨

This incident has niggled at my mind for fifty years and refuses to be forgotten. The kitten could hardly have opened my door and shut it again in the night. The door may even have been locked – I don't remember – but it was certainly shut tight. In my new spirit of facing the facts, no matter how unpalatable I find them, I have to accept that the ginger kitten which appeared and disappeared in Bristol was the ghost of Sandy come to see me before continuing his journey into the afterlife.

As it happens, in this case even the Church of England with its appointed exorcists wouldn't accept a kitten ghost; our curate at St Philip's told us during our confirmation classes that animals don't have souls, and I think their theology holds that you have to have a soul to be a ghost. Perhaps things have changed since I was twelve.

However, the English word 'animal' comes from the Latin *anima*, which means 'soul'. Aristotle considered animals and plants to have souls; the soul governed how the organism grew into the form it took. This was taken up by Dr Rupert Sheldrake in the 1980s: he conceived the idea of morphic fields and morphic resonance, which I will return to later in this book.

What's more, *animism* is the term we use to refer to belief in spirits, which appears to predate formal religions and their concept of a god or supreme being ruling over the universe. Roger Clarke in his *A Natural History of Ghosts: 500 Years of Hunting for Proof* comments that people often catch sight of 'a beloved and recently departed cat or dog' and also mentions the fact that pets can sense ghosts. There are apparently countless stories of cats, dogs and, interestingly enough, infants, watching an invisible presence coming down stairs or across a room.

The Buddhist doctrine of *karma* holds that human souls can be reborn as animals, usually because of past misdeeds. Being reborn as an animal is a serious spiritual setback, but animals are clearly understood to have 'souls' in some sense, although the concept in Buddhism is more that of a consciousness than a soul, and Buddhist ghosts have no physical form. The little kitten which came to my room was very much in physical form, not a transparent wraith as the conventional idea of a ghost would require. It purred in my arms, lapped up the milk with its rough little tongue, waggled its ears and left an indentation in the rug where it had lain.

I recounted my inexplicable story of the ginger kitten to my friend Mira, a doctor, and, instead of coming up with some comforting scientific explanation, she proceeded to tell me about an incident she can never forget when she was working in the A&E Department of a hospital, quite early in her medical career.

One night, after settling all the patients, Mira was sitting with the nurses having a coffee break in their room. The door was open and anyone in the corridor was visible from where they were sitting. As they were chatting, they saw an elderly woman they all recognised – a patient who was bed-ridden and in a room set aside for those with terminal illnesses – pass by the door holding her catheter bag in one hand and dragging her drip stand along with the other. They all exclaimed in disbelief – none of them could believe this woman was capable of getting up in her state of health. One of the nurses jumped up and went to help her but was then non-plussed to find there was nobody in the corridor and nowhere the woman could have gone so quickly. She searched for the patient and then looked into the room she had come from. She was lying in her bed, still attached to the drip. The nurse felt her pulse and soon concluded the woman was dead.

The only conclusion that seems possible is that both Sandy and this elderly woman had survived briefly in physical form apart from their dead bodies, with Sandy even reverting to kitten form. This inevitably makes me think of the film, *21 Grams*, the title of which refers to an experiment in 1907 which recorded a loss of 21.3 grams immediately following a person's death, taken to represent the weight of the soul which leaves the body. The Danes famously have a tradition of opening the window when a person is dying to give the soul a way out of the building.

The belief that a person lives on in some form after death goes back to one of the earliest civilisations in Mesopotamia. The dead were said to carry on an existence in an underworld and needed offerings of food and drink from the living. If these were not provided, they might inflict a variety of misfortunes on the living, including illness. The custom of putting food and drink on a grave continues in a number of cultures all over the world; in the Republic of North Macedonia, where I was to live for eighteen years, people also light a cigarette for a deceased smoker to enjoy and leave it at the grave.

Traditional Chinese perform special rituals for the dead because they believe they still exist and can directly affect our material world. The Mexican celebration of the Day of the Dead with its offerings to deceased relatives is traced back to an Aztec festival honouring the dead, presided over by Mictēcacihuātl, the Queen of the Underworld. It used to take place in the summer but was later absorbed into the Christian holidays around Hallowe'en: All Saints' Eve, All Saints' Day and All Souls' Day. It is worth noting that Catholics believe the souls of the dead go to Purgatory and it is the prayers of the living which will help them to proceed to Heaven.

It is a shock to read that the most revered of all physicists, Albert Einstein, said: 'Science without religion is lame: religion without science is blind.' In his book *The God Delusion*, Richard Dawkins, the University of Oxford's Professor for Public Understanding of Science from 1995 until 2008, persuasively argues – by quoting other statements by the great physicist – that the 'religion' and the 'God' which Einstein and other famous scientists like Carl Sagan and Stephen Hawking have talked about are not the conventional concepts we might assume. Dawkins quotes Einstein again to explain what they mean:

'To sense that behind anything that can be experienced there is something that our mind cannot grasp and whose beauty and sublimity reaches us only indirectly and as a feeble reflection, this is religiousness. In this sense I am religious.'

Dawkins himself says he is religious in this sense, too, 'with the reservation that 'cannot grasp' does not have to mean 'forever ungraspable'. As he notes, using the terms 'religious' and 'God' is too confusing where atheists are concerned.

When it comes to ghosts, however, Dawkins dismisses ghosts as hallucinations of some form or another. This is appropriate to the cases he himself has experienced but it isn't very helpful to my investigation: the ginger kitten and the elderly woman were very real physical manifestations. In neither case did the people seeing them think there was anything 'spooky' or strange about them. Perhaps precisely because it is a unanimous tenet of all religions that we have some kind of consciousness which survives after death, Professor Dawkins has rejected the highly credible sightings of ghosts over thousands of years alongside other beliefs which are clearly much more tenuous, such as virgin birth, or bread and wine turning into flesh and blood.

So, religions all believe in life after death, while mainstream science denies it could exist. We all know what problems scientists had with the Church four hundred years ago in Europe: Giordano Bruno burnt at the stake for not adhering to the Church's views, and Galileo famously having to recant his heretical notion that the Earth and other planets revolved around the Sun.

After Descartes separated Mind from Matter in the seventeenth century, physicists seem to have been happy to leave Mind in all forms to religion while investigating Matter. Sadly, this means that many of them have now become as fixed in their views of what science can study as the Church was in the Middle Ages. And this attitude has been transferred to atheists like me, who don't want to give any consideration to a notion like the afterlife, which has become the exclusive property of religion. This means that anyone in my position of having apparent proof that ghosts exist must look at a fringe area of science to examine this: it is called paraphysics.

One of the few paraphysicists who seems to have any publications to his name is James E. Beichler, author of *Paraphysical Principles of Natural Philosophy.* As was only to be expected, Prof. Beichler was forced out of university teaching in the USA by colleagues who persuaded the university authorities that his research and publications were only 'circuitously related' to the physics he taught.

Prof. Beichler has also written *To Die For: The physical reality of conscious survival,* clearly particularly relevant to ghosts. Beichler makes clear distinctions between LIFE and the BIOFIELD, which are material concepts to do with our bodies, and MIND and CONSCIOUSNESS, which are physical but immaterial and exist in the fifth dimension. MIND and CONSCIOUSNESS are connected to the four-dimensional material world by LIFE but do not die with the body as they inhabit the fifth dimension.

Beichler doesn't like the terms 'soul', 'spirit' or 'ghost' because of the preconceptions which go with them – this deprives them of any objective scientific value according to him. Instead, he uses 'the MIND / CONSCIOUSNESS structure or complex'. He spends some time trying to explain what the fifth dimension might look like, but it takes someone with a better grasp of spatial awareness than me to appreciate it. The key point to understand, however, is that the fourth dimension is space-time and the fifth, according to Beichler, is 'the precursor to all other physical fields – matter, gravity, electricity, magnetism and the other natural fields within our relativistic four-dimensional continuum. Each common physical field is a particular construction of the five-dimensional single field as experienced within our four-dimensional space-time.'

Scenes from the 2014 film *Interstellar* starring Matthew McConaughey came to mind to try to get my head round this concept. There was talk of beings from the fifth dimension in that film, though they turned out to be another version of ourselves. This had made me think the fifth dimension was more about parallel universes or perhaps about Time. I needed some help from a physicist.

Although 'Establishment' scientists do not investigate phenomena like ghosts, there are mainstream physicists who are willing to keep an open mind and discuss how plausible any paraphysical theories might be. Luckily, I had just such a physicist as a neighbour. His name is Mark Hanson. I got in touch with him and explained my project. Luckily, Mark did not dismiss me as a crank and came round for a cup of tea, generously assuring me after a short conversation that he accepted my experiences as genuine and was willing to act as my adviser on questions of physics.

Mark teaches at the University of Kent and also tutors A Level students. He has an exceptional gift for clearly presenting even the most complex and difficult concepts. He gave me a brief overview at that first meeting of the two pillars of physics: general relativity and quantum mechanics, explaining how the first deals with the very big things and the second with the very small. With that he immediately lifted my head out of the matted undergrowth of all the separate theories I had read about, unable to correlate them, and gave me a bird's eye view from above the forest.

Beichler's book had already informed me that in 1921 Theodor Kaluza added a fifth mathematical dimension to Einstein's four-dimensional space-time continuum in order to unify gravity and electromagnetism as different aspects of a single combined field. This fifth dimension has apparently never been refuted but also never verified. Beichler claims in his 2008 book that 'the Einstein-Kaluza model is the only successful theory to unify gravity and electromagnetism'.

Knowing that Mark was there to warn me off anything which was totally unviable as a theory for supernatural phenomena, I explored the internet for other theories. There was a site called Angels & Ghosts, which sadly doesn't seem to exist anymore. However, it presented a theory that ghosts could be made up of plasma, the fourth state of matter beyond a solid, liquid or gas.

Plasma consists of very high energy non-standard particles called ions and electrons. It is thought to make up most of the matter in the universe, but there are many types of plasma with different characteristics, so ghosts could be a form of plasma we don't yet know about.

Like ghosts, plasma generates electromagnetic fields. It even conducts electricity and radiates electromagnetic waves. Scientists have actually produced a device which can measure the biomagnetic fields our bodies produce. It's called a SQUID (superconducting quantum interference device). This connects to the energy field around our bodies. As I know myself, anyone can train themselves to see the auras around any object, whether animate or inanimate. Everything emits radiation, the amount depending apparently on the heat of the object. Could it also be related to us having a plasma body, which might itself correlate to the ancient idea of the *chakras*, or energy centres of the body?

A site called ParaWiki used to state that ghosts are a 'plasma-based life form that originally existed in symbiosis with a human body, but decoupled from that corporeal form upon its death.' According to this theory, all carbon-based life-forms (all life on Earth) also have a plasma-based (bioplasma) body. Apparently, the locus of our consciousness can switch from our carbon-based body to our bioplasma one – in meditation, for example. In Rapid Eye Movement (REM) sleep, our carbon-based body processes information from our bioplasma body.

Our two bodies are in symbiosis and our bioplasma 'brain' is imprinted with our experience and personality in the same way as our normal brain is.

This imprinting of ourselves on our bodies immediately made me think of the recorded cases of heart transplant patients taking over the likes and dislikes of their respective donors. The best known is probably Claire Sylvia, who writes in her book *A Change of Heart* about her sudden craving for beer and chicken nuggets, favourites of her 18-year-old male donor, who died in a motorcycle accident. This phenomenon is attributed to cell memory and accepted by several scientists and physicians. If there is a real communion between our carbon-based and bioplasma bodies, then it would follow that they both contain the characteristics and experience of their hosts.

This theory of what ghosts are holds that the bioplasma body, being of the same age as our carbon-based body, normally dies at the same time or shortly afterwards, but that it sometimes survives and decouples, especially in cases of premature death by accident.

There's the famous 1893 case of Vice-Admiral Sir George Tryon, who was seen walking through his home in full-dress uniform by the guests at his wife's tea party. He was in fact several thousand miles away off the coast of Syria. He drowned when his ship sank in a collision on manoeuvres at the time when witnesses saw him in England.

Interestingly enough, the idea of us having two 'bodies' ties in very well with the Ancient Chinese belief in two souls. According to this, human beings all have a *po,* an earth soul existing from conception, and a *hun*, which comes into being at birth and is made of *ch'i*, the life force. At death, the *hun* leaves the body while the *po* remains.

The Ancient Egyptians believed there were *six* parts to the human being and followed mummification procedures very carefully, as each part had to be preserved for the person to proceed to the afterlife. The *ka* was a duplicate of the body and needed food and other offerings to use on its journey. This 'body double' coincides exactly with the ginger kitten, the elderly woman and the vice-admiral.

Interestingly, the Ancient Greeks also distinguished what we might call another body, separate from the soul, and they called it a 'daemon'(*δαιμόνιον*). It is a higher part of ourselves, which inspires us. Socrates is said to have consulted his daemon, especially in matters of philosophy (Plutarch's essay entitled 'A Discourse Concerning Socrates's Daemon') although, for him, it appears to be more what we might term his conscience. According to Steve Richards, author of *The Traveller's Guide to the Astral Plane*, 'the 'daemon', if you will, is the 'still, small voice' from within.'

Anyone who has read Pullman's *His Dark Materials* will, of course, recognise this daemon as a separate body from ourselves (normally some kind of animal), which is yet an integral and vital part of us. In Pullman's fictional world, if our daemon is parted from us, we become like zombies.

Another interesting feature of the apparition of the kitten ghost is that, shortly after its death, it came more than a hundred miles to find me in a place where it had never been. Distance and time did not apply, only the telepathic bond between Sandy and me. The same phenomenon applied to the ghost of Sir George Tryon, which was seen in his house, his family home, at the time of his death in a ship thousands of miles away. This suggests that these apparitions must operate in a different dimension of some kind, though the elderly woman patient my friend Mira saw remained in the hospital.

Nevertheless, what all the ghosts concerned here have in common is that they only had a fleeting time of existence. They all appear to have vanished after a short time. Did they cease to exist or did they become invisible? I'll come back to this with a later experience apparently proving the existence of invisible spirits of the dead around us.

Something else which fascinates me about two of the ghosts I've cited here is that they didn't manifest in exactly the same form as their dead bodies: Sandy came in kitten form and Sir George in full dress uniform. Is our 'body double' some kind of ideal form we have of ourselves? Was Sandy always a kitten at heart? Did the Vice-Admiral value above all his rank and status?

It is interesting that the elderly woman patient who died in hospital was in the form in which she had died, in her hospital gown holding her catheter bag and dragging along her drip stand. This has echoes of the first English ghost story ever published, *A True Relation of the Apparition of one Mrs Veal, the Next Day after Her Death, to one Mrs Bargrave, at Canterbury* of 1706. There is no reason to believe that it is anything but a true account.

On Saturday, 8th September 1705 at midday Mrs Bargrave heard the rustle of a dress as she was sitting in her small house and looked up to see her friend Mrs Veal, who had appeared quite unannounced. She was wearing her nightclothes with a hood and a silk handkerchief tied round her throat. Mrs Bargrave was too polite to observe this lack of decorum in her guest, who sat down and started chatting in the most natural of ways. She did, however, comment on the copy of Charles Drelincourt's *Discourse Against the Fear of Death* which she saw lying on the windowsill: she said it was the truth.

In a conversation that lasted nearly an hour and three-quarters, Mrs Veal eventually got round to the reason for her visit, which was to ask Mrs Bargrave to write to certain people, making sure they were aware of the bequests she had made them in her will. She seemed anxious that her brother might not carry out her final wishes. Mrs Bargrave saw her friend off at the front door and only discovered the following day from an undertaker that Mrs Veal had in fact died at noon the day before she had visited her friend. Apart from her unusual clothes for paying visits, Mrs Veal had clearly not awakened any doubt in Mrs Bargrave that her friend was not a living, breathing person.

☙

I've lived for many years with the kind of contradiction Harari writes is so human in his *Sapiens: A Brief History of Humankind*. My own experience has shown me that human beings must be more than a combination of chemicals and yet I have professed that belief. Now I come to examine what ghosts are, I find it intuitively right that they must have something to do with what has always been called the soul, which, again, must relate to consciousness in some way.

As a linguist, I find it interesting that the words for 'soul' in Greek and Latin originally meant 'breath' or 'wind', air in motion. This is also true of the Hebrew word *ruakh*. Greek and Latin developed different words in their literary languages for 'breath', 'soul' and 'wind', while the Hebrew continued to have all three meanings. The Chinese concept of *ch'i*, the life force, means 'the original breath'. As early as the sixth century BCE, the Greek philosopher Anaximenes identified the air all around us with the air which was the basis of an individual's life: 'Just as our soul, being air, holds us together, so do breath and air encompass the whole world.'[1] Nowadays we would be more likely to talk about energy rather than air, but the association of our essence with that of the universe is still the same.

I'll leave this examination of what apparitions consist of with these ideas in mind: human beings and animals must have at least one other invisible part to them, an immaterial body of some kind, perhaps made of dark energy, which operates in a different dimension from the ones in which we normally operate. After death, this body can sometimes materialise in physical form in our world for a brief period.

---

1. *Symbolism and Belief* by Edwyn Bevan, first published by George Allen & Unwin Ltd, 1938, p.154

2.

Auntie Dorothy's dream: 1970
Prophetic dreams and Time

Because people who adopt a scientific world view have a commitment to building on the scientific ideas currently thought to account best for natural phenomena, it is not surprising they would prefer more mundane explanations, such as coincidence, for any seeming premonitions found in dreams.

G.W. Domhoff, *Dreams and Parapsychology*

My godmother was a frequent visitor to our house while I was growing up. She was Dorothy Bone, my mother's closest friend from her childhood in Kettering. She still lived there, whereas we had moved to Leicester, 28 miles away, when I was just one year old, as Dad had got a job at the East Midlands Gas Board based in the city.

Auntie Dorothy was a classic beauty with fine features and wavy brown hair. She looked like Celia Johnson in *Brief Encounter*, except she had a stronger face with more of a square jaw. Her husband was a car mechanic with his own business, which she ran for him – one woman who had managed to go on working after marriage in the 1950s. It seems that was respectable enough if it was a family business and there were no children to look after.

I think Auntie Dorothy took her godmothering duties with

me more seriously than she might have done if she'd had children of her own; that was not to be. Then her husband died in a motorcycle accident. Auntie Dorothy didn't retire into a bleak widowhood but threw herself into the business. She must have been the only woman garage owner for miles around, but she had built up a reputation for efficiency and honesty; the business grew and made money. We saw less of her in those years, but she would turn up from time to time, driving her own car, a smart black one, which was no doubt in excellent condition. To me, she was the height of sophistication, matched only by my father's sister, Auntie Frances, who drank gin and tonics.

Auntie Dorothy came for my confirmation, of course, presenting me with a red leather Book of Common Prayer in a gold cardboard box. It isn't the English way to talk about religion – it's much too embarrassing – so I have no way of knowing how much Auntie Dorothy believed in Church of England teachings.

On her visits Auntie Dorothy always had a beatific smile for me and never complained about loneliness or emptiness or depression, at least not in my hearing. In middle age she gave up her business and went to work as a receptionist in a doctor's surgery. I don't know why that happened. Had she tired of dealing with men in dirty overalls smelling of engine oil, or was it the male customers making passes that finally made her give it all up? Perhaps the business just stopped doing so well for some reason. Perhaps she was in love with the doctor whose surgery she now ran. She never remarried, though.

It was when I came home from Bristol for the vacation in my second year of university that Auntie Dorothy came to stay and told me about her dream, the one I have never forgotten. It was about Joyce. Mum wasn't the only one of Auntie Dorothy's friends who'd moved away from Kettering. There was also Joyce, who'd gone much further away. Her father had gone to work for Morris Motors in Cowley. Auntie Dorothy and Joyce had more or less lost touch except for Christmas cards. But one night Auntie Dorothy had a dream about Joyce which was so vivid she remembered every detail of it when she woke up.

In the dream, Joyce was to be married to a man she had only known for six weeks. Auntie Dorothy waited for the bride in the Victorian church on the Cowley Road where the wedding was to take place. The Wedding March thundered out from the organ and Joyce began her walk down the aisle on her father's arm. She was wearing a long white satin dress with a fitted bodice, lace modestly hiding her cleavage and her shoulders, forming loose short sleeves, the full skirt bushing out from the waist with several layers of stiff petticoats underneath. Her net veil reached her shoulders and was crowned by a pearl tiara. She was holding a bouquet of white roses.

When the service was over, Auntie Dorothy got a good look at the groom as the married couple walked up the aisle. He was quite a striking man, tall and slightly stooped with greying black hair and shy brown eyes. He was clearly a retiring man who hated being the centre of attention but glowed next to Joyce, much in love. The reception took place in an old hotel with a grand staircase and mock Tudor beams. There was prawn cocktail, poached salmon and sherry trifle for the wedding breakfast. Joyce made the rounds of the tables and came to Auntie Dorothy, who was sitting alone surveying the scene.

'Well, here's Dorothy Bone, clairvoyant,' she commented and squeezed her friend's shoulder happily before moving on.

The cake was cut and pieces distributed. The newly-weds went upstairs to change into their going-away outfits. They were off to Weston-super-Mare for a week's honeymoon. When they re-emerged, Joyce was wearing a pink Jackie-Kennedy pillbox hat with her pink double-breasted jacket and pencil skirt. She looked a little uncomfortable – this wasn't the kind of thing she usually wore; she was more a sensible-dress-and-cardigan sort of person. Anyway, the happy couple drove off in the suitably decorated car with its Just Married sign on the back and the attached tin cans rattling away down the road.

Auntie Dorothy woke up and after breakfast wrote to Joyce, telling her she had dreamt she was getting married to a man she had only known for six weeks. The dream had been so real that Auntie Dorothy was sure she must have somehow seen what had happened to her friend. A few days later there was a reply.

'If only . . .' Joyce wrote. 'How romantic it all sounds, marrying a man I'd only known for six weeks. How strange you should dream such a thing about me . . .'

Auntie Dorothy shrugged and agreed: how strange indeed. She quickly forgot about Joyce and the dream during her busy days at the doctor's surgery.

It was six months later when she received a letter, addressed in Joyce's handwriting, to Mrs D. Bone, Clairvoyant. Sure enough, Auntie Dorothy's friend had had a whirlwind romance and was inviting her old friend to her wedding a week on Saturday.

Auntie Dorothy was too spooked to accept the wedding invitation but Joyce didn't give up. She sent her some of the wedding photos.

'Is this the man you saw?' she asked. 'Is this the dress I wore in your dream? How about my going-away outfit?'

Yes, everything was exactly as it had been in the dream.

❧

Aristotle states: 'Most prophetic dreams are . . . to be classed as mere coincidences, especially all such as are extravagant, and those in the fulfilment of which the dreamers have no initiative, such as in the case of a sea-fight, or of things taking place far away.'

Rather hard to put this down to a coincidence, I feel. Perhaps if Auntie Dorothy had dreamt about her friend Joyce getting married, but without the specific and unusual detail that she had only known the groom for six weeks, it might be easier to dismiss. Correctly seeing what he looked like and the clothes the bride and groom were wearing is really stretching the idea that coincidence is involved. No, we have to accept, *pace* Aristotle, that Auntie Dorothy did have a prophetic dream and that the future can be foretold. This brings up the knotty problem of our lives being mapped out for us already, and the even knottier problems of the subconscious and what Time is.

In *About Time: Einstein's Unfinished Revolution*, Paul Davies writes: 'Until we have a firm understanding of the flow of time, or incontrovertible evidence that it is indeed an illusion, then we will not know who we are, or what part we are playing in the great cosmic drama.' This is the crux of the matter: we know that time is a relative concept, but this fact is entirely at odds with our own everyday experience of it as measured by clocks. How do we make the leap to viewing time from a completely different perspective, which would make it perfectly acceptable that, in her dream, Auntie Dorothy fast-forwarded to an event six months hence?

H. G. Wells's *The Time Machine*, written in 1895, was not the first work of fiction to express the human desire to experience the attraction and thrill of liberating ourselves from the restraints of time and space. The first was apparently *Memoirs of the Twentieth Century* by Samuel Madden, written in 1733, and time travel has been a popular plot theme from Dickens's *A Christmas Carol* of 1843 to Frank Capra's 1946 film *It's a Wonderful Life* and Terry Gilliam's masterful *12 Monkeys* from 1995, not to mention *The Terminator* series or *Back to the Future*. However, all this science fiction concerns travelling back to the *past*, which involves going through a wormhole. The American physicist Michio Kaku tells us we would have to wait for a Theory of Everything to do this, as the combination of Einstein's theory of relativity with the quantum theory of radiation, which would have to occur to make this possible, '...yields a series of infinite answers that are meaningless.'

On the other hand, Sean Carroll, theoretical physicist and author of *From Eternity to Here: The Quest for the Ultimate Theory of Time*, says that 'The weird thing about the arrow of time is that it's not to be found in the underlying laws of physics. It's not there. So it's a feature of the universe we see, but not a feature of the laws of the individual particles. So the arrow of time is built on top of whatever local laws of physics apply.' In our universe, the arrow of time always moves forward, from the past into the future.

We have all imbibed enough science fiction, even if we're not Star Trek or Dr Who aficionados, to know that people on a spaceship, for example, experience time completely differently from those back on Earth as they speed away from our planet; human beings on a space exploration trip might return to Earth a few years older while their schoolmates are long dead, and centuries have passed. So time travel into the *future* is perfectly possible and in fact occurs. The world record for travelling into the future is currently held by Russian cosmonaut Gennady Padalka, who has orbited the Earth for 879 days and has hence travelled more than 0.04 seconds into his own future.

Another important factor here seems to me to be the arbitrary nature of Auntie Dorothy's dream: she had never had a prophetic dream like this, or had one afterwards, to my knowledge. It was also about somebody she was no longer particularly close to, and who she hadn't seen or thought about for some time. In other words, it was complete chance that she should foresee a future event. It is as if she tuned into a normally inaccessible channel of reality operating on a different time-scale, perhaps via her bioplasma body, if we accept the theory from the last chapter.

Gordon Smith, a respected British medium, says that 'more often than not, when a person gets a glimpse of something in the future, it is random rather than deliberate. This type of vision may occur when the person is in a dream state. When you are in such a state, your mind is between worlds: the world of the spirit, as your spirit returns there when the body sleeps, and the physical world which you are returning to. In this spirit world, there is no time whatsoever, and in a state of no time, one can look in all directions of time, past, present and future. So when the consciousness is returning to the human state, it may remember a glimpse of the future.'

I am finally coming to realise the full amplitude of the

research I have taken on in this book: when considering Auntie Dorothy's dream, it involves trying to come to terms with three concepts which have never been agreed upon in human experience, namely consciousness, sleep and dreams.

There is no consensus whatsoever about what consciousness is. For example, the eminent mathematical physicist Sir Roger Penrose developed a theory based on the observations of unconscious patients by Stuart Hameroff, an anaesthesiologist, linking consciousness with quantum mechanics. His colleague, Stephen Hawking of *A Brief History of Time* fame, another physicist hailed as a genius, wrote: 'I get uneasy when people, especially theoretical physicists, talk about consciousness. His argument seemed to be that consciousness is a mystery and quantum gravity is another mystery so they must be related.'

Yet another famous scientist, Francis Crick, one of the co-discoverers of the molecular structure of DNA, for which he received the Nobel Prize alongside James Watson and Maurice Wilkins, wrote *The Astonishing Hypothesis - The Scientific Search for the Soul* in 1994. Crick states that his main aim in writing the book is to encourage scientists to do a proper, scientifically grounded investigation into consciousness and to encourage other researchers in their turn to take account of neuroscientific breakthroughs.

As I mentioned before, ever since Descartes made a division between Mind and Matter, scientists have been content to deal with Matter and leave Mind to religion. When psychology came on the scene in the late nineteenth century to deal with Mind, it was relegated to the fringes of science and not really considered sufficiently 'scientific' in its methods. As for parapsychology, which appeared in the 1930s and examined extrasensory perception, it has never been taken seriously by 'proper' scientists, despite results which statisticians regard as impressive. Even the great Hawking obviously felt that scientists had no business investigating non-material phenomena.

When it comes to sleep, I have thought much more about it since entering the menopause and having trouble achieving a sleeping state. You can read any number of accounts of what happens during sleep, of how it is vital for maintaining our endocrine and immune systems, but the only way it is described is some kind of 'altered consciousness'; since we don't know what consciousness is, that's not very helpful. My husband referred to having a siesta as 'touching the unconscious'. Perhaps he should have said 'touching consciousness'. No one seems to deal with what happens in that elusive magic moment of falling asleep, which none of us seems able to conjure at will. We don't appear to have access to a 'switch' to bring on sleep immediately.

'To sleep, perchance to dream'[2] – but, again, no one can tell you what dreams are. There are any number of theories of what they might *mean*, but not what they actually *are*. There is a field of study called oneirology which does research on dreams, and you will find the following description at Schneider, A., & Domhoff, G. W. (2018) 'The Quantitative Study of Dreams' Retrieved March 18, 2018 from http://www.dreamresearch.net/: 'So, to sum it all up, we can think of a 'dream' as a report of a memory of a cognitive experience that happens under the kinds of conditions that are most frequently produced in a state called 'sleep.' But if you want it to be more simple,

---

2.   William Shakespeare, *Hamlet*, Act III, Scene 1

you can think of dreams as the little dramas our minds make up when the 'self' system is not keeping us alert to the world around us.' Presumably, the 'self' system referred to here is what others might call consciousness. This is interesting, as the theory of us having another 'body' stated that in REM (Rapid Eye Movement) sleep, ie when dreaming, our carbon-based body processes information from our bioplasma body. This bioplasma body might also be referred to as our consciousness.

Annie Besant is clear what happens: 'In sleep, the astral body, enveloping the consciousness, slips out of the physical vehicle, leaving the dense and etheric bodies to slumber.'[3]

When it comes to prophetic dreams, the explanation offered by a researcher on dreaming is unashamedly circular: 'First, paranormal explanations are incompatible with the naturalistic view of the world developed in the physical sciences over the past few hundred years. Telepathy, precognition, and other paranormal hypotheses are not credible from this perspective because they do not fit with established physical science explanations, the occasional appeals to either relativity theory or quantum physics by some parapsychologists notwithstanding. Because people who adopt a scientific world view have a commitment to building on the scientific ideas currently thought to account best for natural phenomena, it is not surprising they would prefer more mundane explanations, such as coincidence, for any seeming premonitions found in dreams.' (Domhoff, G. W. (2000). *Dreams and Parapsychology*. Retrieved from the World Wide Web: http://www.dreamresearch.net/Library/domhoff_2000c.html)

---

3.   *The Ancient Wisdom*, p.83

How science is ever to progress if it is only to work with 'established physical science explanations' does not seem to be of concern. It is well over a century since Albert Einstein himself described the idea of 'thought experiments' by which he arrived at the theory of relativity, as my neighbour Mark explained to me. Obviously, any scientist who addresses any area concerned with consciousness, sleep or dreams will be required to use Einstein's approach. Science should involve the search for knowledge, not the kind of sticking to dogma usually associated with religion. It really does seem that many scientists are taking over the role the Church previously took towards science in refusing to even consider any phenomena which lie outside what they have termed 'normal'.

So I am left with my own thoughts on prophetic dreams like the one my Auntie Dorothy clearly experienced. We are all aware that the dream state gives us a different perception of reality, one where clock time doesn't apply, as if one is step-ping outside the timeline which usually holds us in its grasp. Perhaps this can happen in a different dimension, where we can actually witness future events. Most scientists appear agreed about 'the block universe'. This contains everything that has ever existed, exists and will exist. Just as when I am in one place, I know there are so many other places which exist where I could be, so I can only be in the present, although all the past and all of the future are out there already in space-time. Having a prophetic dream must mean we somehow leave our present viewpoint and glimpse the future in the block of space-time, but this only happens in our sleep. The strong implication is that we do inhabit a different dimension in that state.

The theory of 'the block universe' does, of course, pose a problem for anyone who wants to believe in free will, as it means our lives are already mapped out – we can't change what has happened or will happen. This is interesting when we consider what effect Auntie Dorothy's dream may have had on Joyce. When she met a man who quickly proposed to her, did she reflect that the dream was coming true? Did she make a genuine choice to marry this man or did she subconsciously think it was 'meant to be' and therefore went along with it? We have no way of knowing how much or how little she may have been affected by the prophetic dream her friend had had about her.

3.

Mystery in the Finnish woods: 1971
Telepathic pain, extrasensory perception, psi

The test of a theory is its ability to cope with all the relevant phenomena, not its a priori 'reasonableness'. The latter would have proved a poor guide in the development of science, which often makes progress by its encounter with the totally unexpected and initially extremely puzzling.

JOHN CHARLTON POLKINGHORNE, *THE PARTICLE PLAY*

I assume that the reader is familiar with the idea of extrasensory perception, and the meaning of the four items of it, viz telepathy, clairvoyance, precognition and psychokinesis. These disturbing phenomena seem to deny all our usual scientific ideas. How we should like to discredit them! Unfortunately, the statistical evidence, at least for telepathy, is overwhelming.

ALAN TURING, 'COMPUTING MACHINERY AND INTELLIGENCE',
MIND, 59, 433-460

After three years at university studying French, the only job I knew I didn't want to do was teaching French, so I looked around for something else. There were plenty of interesting posts for graduates in those days and I ended up applying for one of the forty-odd positions advertised by The British Council for English teachers with Finnish-British Societies in Finland. You didn't need any kind of teaching experience. They interviewed me and offered me the post in Kauttua, a small settlement in the south-west of the country.

I had never been particularly attracted to Nordic lands, being a lover of sun and sea, but I thought this job would give me plenty of free time and solitude to write the great novel I was destined to produce. Finland would be the perfect setting to write, uninhibited by family or friends – the modern-day equivalent of a garret for the struggling Romantic writer.

The Society gave me a room in a typical wooden house with five other young women who worked for the paper mill. It was about the same size as my room in Bristol but, unlike that one, it boasted double glazing and central heating. My furniture was the equivalent of what Ikea still produces today: simple, functional and elegant.

Kauttua existed because of the paper mill. All the buildings belonged to the mill and all the homes housed people who worked there. But the whole settlement was located in the woods, where the mill wasn't visible, and the buildings were very spread out with plenty of space between them. It felt as if you were living in the countryside. There was a lake nearby and the pinewoods stretched for miles and miles around.

My job at the Finnish-British Society had sounded easy: giving English conversation classes. My very first class soon revealed the difficulty of the task I had taken on. I had four participants, all men in their late thirties (I thought they were all middle-aged at the time, so I'm now recalculating). They all worked at the paper mill, of course, some sort of engineers.

We sat around in a downstairs room in the clubhouse on green armchairs. I expected this to be a relaxing setting, conducive to plenty of conversation, much better than having a classroom with desks and chairs. I must say, just getting their names and jobs out of them proved challenging, but I was undaunted and went on to ask them about their interests.

'What do you do in your spare time?' got no reply so I changed it to 'What do you do in your free time?' in case 'spare' wasn't a word they knew. Still no response from any of them, even when asked individually. When I was just beginning to break out in a cold sweat, Kari finally said, so softly I had to ask him to repeat the word: 'Filmi.'

'Ah!' I said so loudly they all jumped, 'Films? You like films?'

Kari nodded rather uncertainly, clearly wary of setting off any more enthusiastic exclamations on my part.

'What kind of films do you like?' I asked, leaning forward in a way I later learnt from experience was bound to cause alarm.

Kari cast his eyes down to the floor to consider the rather unprepossessing green carpet they all seemed to find fascinating. They appeared to have been caught in a freeze frame which didn't affect me. I felt I'd become part of a terribly avant-garde theatre performance.

'Action films?' I ploughed on, 'Thrillers? Horror? Comedies? Romance...?'

It was like watching a film on the internet today when it stops and that revolving circle comes on in the middle of the screen while the system reboots itself, or whatever it does, except my feeling wasn't one of annoyance but of mounting panic.

All the English teachers who had come out to Finland with me were experiencing the same Finnish reticence among the majority of their students. Consequently, we came to spend every weekend visiting each other, just so we could have a normal conversation in our native tongue. During the week, I had too much time to feel lonely and to question where my life was going.

Part of my angst was probably connected to Mum. When I had been in Paris, she had had a nervous breakdown, which I only heard about from Auntie Dorothy some time later. Mum would never have dreamt of asking me not to go to Paris or of making me aware how my absence affected her. The only hint I had had was seeing her burst into tears when I looked back at her at the airport.

Mum had been a very competent secretary to a firm of architects before the War, and had worked in a bank during the day and in a servicemen's canteen in the evenings during the War. She had married Dad in a flush of romance soon after war was declared in September 1939, just before he went off to man the searchlights in Norfolk. It was a full five years later when Dad came back home, by then a Major in the Indian Army. He had organised and dropped supplies to troops in the Burmese jungle fighting the Japanese. He resumed his job in purchasing at the Corby iron and steel works, but there was no question of Mum working. Married women didn't have careers in those days.

When I left home, Mum had to face the emptiness of her life. She went into a steady decline, plagued by arthritis, high blood pressure and heart disease. Mrs King, my best friend Annette's mother, knew who was responsible.

'All this gadding about abroad,' she said to me. 'How can you do this to your mother?'

My pangs of guilt were relegated to my subconscious. Mum

would always insist that I had to live my own life and go wherever it took me. She was the selfless, self-sacrificing type, and was determined that I should have the career she had been denied. She encouraged me to do all the things she had never done: staying on at school, going to university, travelling. I had no secrets from her – I would tell her everything I felt, everything I wished for, everything I dreamt about. I knew she lived through me in a certain sense and that I owed her a full account. We carried on our conversations by letter, wherever I was, replying to each other by return, which meant I would get a letter once a week in Finland.

One evening, I was walking back to my house after a class at the club house. I was going at my usual fast pace, not afraid of slipping on the shiny snow-covered path in my warm boots, lined with faux fur and with excellent grip on the soles. Suddenly, I felt a tremendous pain in my right hip, so intense I collapsed on the ground. I lay there nonplussed for a while, holding onto my hip and breathing deeply.

There was no question of being able to get up, so I started slowly pulling myself along on my left side towards the house. Luckily, I wasn't too far away by then. There were no lights on – no one else was home yet. I crawled up the steps and unlocked the door on my knees. My room was first on the right and I staggered in and lay on my bed. The excruciating pain gradually subsided and I decided I would find out about a doctor I could visit the next day rather than calling someone to take me to A&E. I managed to make myself a snack for supper and then had an early night.

The following morning, I woke up and got out of bed. I was brushing my teeth before I remembered the previous evening's pain. There wasn't a trace of it. I pressed my right hip gently in various places – nothing hurt. I had a busy day of classes ahead, so I didn't ask anyone about seeing a doctor. As a week went by without any recurrence of the pain, I began to put it out of my mind and forget about it. What worried me, though, was that there was no letter from Mum on the day I expected it. Still no letter the next day, or the next, or the one following that. Finally, a letter arrived, but the address was written in Dad's handwriting. I ripped open the envelope with great trepidation.

'Don't worry, duckie,' Dad had written, 'Mum's in hospital but I'm sure she'll be better soon. She finally had the second hip replacement she was waiting for, but it didn't go too smoothly this time because she had a heart attack during the operation. This meant she couldn't get up and walk about as quickly as she was supposed to afterwards. When she finally did get out of bed, putting pressure on her hip fractured her pelvis and now she has to stay in hospital for a while for it to mend . . .'

Just reading about the fracture of Mum's pelvis brought back that agonising pain in my hip. I sat down and wrote straight back to Dad. When did this happen exactly? I sent all my love to my Mum and told Dad to let me know how she was every day. I waited impatiently for his reply.

Sure enough, the day and the time of Mum's pelvic fracture coincided with the unexplained pain that I had experienced.

❧

This particular paranormal occurrence seems to me much more open to scientific explanation than the ginger kitten. I remember hearing on BBC Radio Four some years ago about an experiment that had been done with a mother mouse and her baby. The two had been separated and the baby mouse taken to a laboratory a hundred miles away. There it had been subjected to pain for short isolated periods of time. The scientists monitoring the mother mouse in the other distant laboratory had recorded sudden expressions of severe alarm in her at the exact moments when her baby would have been in pain.

I have been unable to trace this experiment now I'm writing this book, but have been told by academics that it must have been one carried out in the Soviet Union. Some such experiments, not including this one, are described in *Psychic Discoveries Behind the Iron Curtain*, but these have mainly been dismissed as flawed by Western scientists. My memory is so clear of the experiment described on the radio because the similarity with my own experience of my mother's pain being relayed to me struck me so forcibly.

An experiment which showed mice felt each other's pain was carried out by Andrey Ryabinin, a behavioural neuroscientist at Oregon Health & Science University in Portland in 2016. This transferral of pain only seemed to take place when the mice were in separate cages in the same room together. It didn't occur when they were in different rooms, so this experiment didn't really parallel my own experience as did the untraceable one I heard about on the radio.

I understand that many pharmaceutical experiments are done on mice because they share more than 95 percent of our human genome and get most of the same diseases, for many of the same genetic reasons. Therefore, the results of mouse experiments often correlate to human biology. Hence it seems to me perfectly logical that pain can be transmitted telepathically between human beings in the same way as it is between mice, especially when there is such a close genetic tie as between a mother and her daughter.

My friend Dragana, now an eminent specialist in genetics at two of the great London teaching hospitals, told me about a telepathic incident with her own mother, who was ill in hospital. One morning she was woken up by her mother shouting 'Dragana! Come!' She rushed to the hospital to see her mother, who died that night. Dragana would not have seen her before she died had it not been for that call from her mother she distinctly heard.

On another occasion, she had a freak accident with her own daughter. Dragana was in the kitchen holding a pan when Teona rushed in saying she'd had enough of studying. She flung herself at her mother in mock anguish, but Dragana lost her balance and fell on the floor, hitting her head on the wall, with Teona falling on top of her. Teona got to her feet but was horrified to find that Dragana just lay there, unable to move or speak. Out of her mind with concern, she called 999 and the ambulance came quickly.

Although she couldn't speak, Dragana was very aware of everything that was going on. She could see herself lying there in the ambulance and thought she was dying. All she could focus on was how Teona would be feeling, how she would never forgive herself for causing her mother's death. Dragana knew the ambulance would take her to Pembury Hospital, where there was no surgeon skilled enough to help her. She thought they must take her to King's College Hospital, where she knew the surgeons who could save her, but, of course, she was incapable of speech and of telling the ambulance staff this. However, it seemed Teona could hear her thoughts. Dragana's daughter said:

'It's OK, Mum, I'll tell them to take you to King's.'

One of the most impressive experiments in telepathy was carried out just before World War II by Sir Hubert Wilkins and Harold Sherman. Wilkins was an Australian photographer and naturalist famous for exploration using airplanes and submarines. The Russian government asked him to find one of their planes which had been lost somewhere in the Arctic off the coast of Canada. Sherman was a popular writer interested in psychic phenomena. The two men decided to use this opportunity to see if Sherman could use telepathy to know what Wilkins was doing in the Arctic. Both kept a log so they could compare Wilkins's activities with Sherman's perceptions, which were written down and handed to third-party witnesses long before Wilkins's log could be seen.

The most striking similarity of many in the logs kept by the two occurred on 30th November 1938. Wilkins was in Aklavik in the Canadian North West Territories, in the middle of nowhere above the Arctic Circle. The team were invited to a party at the local hospital in the small settlement. During the party, two of the men went to the basement where they found ping-pong tables. They had a great time playing the game with some nurses. That evening back in New York, Sherman recorded a strong impression of ping-pong balls and wrote: 'Is there a table in town where people play?'

Minor telepathic incidents, such as thinking about someone just before they call you, are too commonplace to recount and it has happened several times in my life that I pick up the phone to call a close relative at the exact moment when they are doing the same thing. Many people have had that experience, too.

Rupert Sheldrake is an outstanding biologist, who has investigated phenomenal aspects of animal behaviour, such as how pigeons find their way home, the telepathic abilities of dogs, cats and other animals, and the apparent abilities of animals to anticipate earthquakes and tsunamis. He subsequently studied similar phenomena in people, including the sense of being stared at, telepathy between mothers and babies, telepathy in connection with telephone calls, and premonitions. As a biologist, he bases his research on natural history and experiments under natural conditions rather than laboratory studies.

Sheldrake has a computerised database of 5,000 case histories of apparently unexplained perceptiveness by people and non-human animals. He has carried out questionnaires on the topic with 2,000 people and, in addition, collated the results of telephone interviews with 2,000 randomly selected people in the UK and USA. What is more, he spent over ten years doing a variety of experiments on the sense of being stared at and various aspects of telepathy before writing his book *The Sense of Being Stared At and Other Aspects of the Extended Mind,* published in 2004. It charts the results of this vast amount of research and concludes that our accepted idea that the mind is in the brain is simply wrong.

He puts forward the idea of the extended mind, which interconnects us all. Our mind has a field which is not confined to the inside of our brain but stretches out way beyond it, rather like magnetic and gravitational fields. He posits that we, alongside other animals, have a seventh sense, which covers telepathy, the sense of being stared at and premonitions. It is in a different category from our other five senses and from the sixth sense already established by biologists working on the electrical and magnetic senses of animals, such as eels and various species of migratory fish and birds, or the heat-sensing organs of some species of snake, or vibration sense of web-weaving spiders.

There is little doubt that telepathy and telepathic pain such as I experienced in the Finnish woods, thousands of miles away from my mother in her Leicester hospital, represent a genuine phenomenon, but one which is very hard to prove by scientific experiment. Nevertheless, Arthur Koestler in *The Roots of Coincidence* does report on the results of such experiments done at American and British universities in the 1930s, which he thought showed beyond doubt that telepathy or extra-sensory perception (ESP) exists. He notes: 'Thus, according to the rules of the game in the exact sciences, the question 'Does ESP exist?' should have been regarded as settled, and the controversy should have shifted to the next problem, 'How does it work?"

More recently, Michael Persinger of the Laurentian University in Ontario has done experiments to simulate temporal lobe seizures, a kind of misfiring of the brain during which sufferers have reported experiences closely resembling the feeling that another being is present, as well as intense religious bliss, sudden overwhelming emotions and numbness, or electrical tickling sensations. Telepaths have apparently also reported such experiences and Persinger has concluded that ESP is consequently due to a misfiring of the brain, like temporal lobe seizures.

However, in 2004 Swedish psychologists reported in the journal *Nature* that they were unable to reproduce Persinger's findings in replicated experiments at the Universities of Uppsala and Lund. Moreover, Persinger himself also carried out experiments with Ingo Swann, a renowned psychic, who demonstrated clear remote viewing expertise under controlled conditions, thus proving that ESP can't be dismissed as the illusion of a misfiring brain.

Harvard psychologist Shelley Carson reported an experiment in 2003 which had been carried out with Harvard undergraduates. It tested their creativity, IQ, personality and latent inhibition. The latter refers to 'the capacity to screen from conscious awareness stimuli previously experienced as irrelevant'[4]. It is what allows us to multi-task: driving a car on a busy road while chatting to a passenger and sipping coffee. We have learned what's important to pay attention to while driving and thus can divide our attention between various things when there are no hazards in sight.

Healthy people have high latent inhibition, remaining stable and focussed on only what matters, while low latent inhibition can be a symptom of schizophrenia, seeing meaningful relationships everywhere where none exist. Nobel Prize Winner John Nash, the subject of the film *A Beautiful Mind*, 'saw the world in a way no one could have imagined', as the film's tag line announced. In Carson's experiment, students who were highly creative and highly intelligent also had significantly lower latent inhibition. Such people also report more psychic experiences. This may well be linked to the fact that they pay more attention to what is happening around them, are more open to experience and thinking 'outside the box'.

The biologist Berthold P. Wiesner decided a special term was required to refer to the unknown factor some people exhibit in extrasensory perception; he called it 'psi' after the 23rd

---

4.   Carson (2003) Abstract

letter of the Greek alphabet, the initial letter of the Greek word *psyche*, meaning 'mind' or 'soul'. It was first used by psychologist Robert Thouless in a 1942 article published in the *British Journal of Psychology*. Psi has been divided into two major categories: mind-to-mind (mental) and mind-to-matter (physical). Mind-to-mind psi covers telepathy, while mind-to-matter covers telekinesis, moving things through the power of the mind without touching them. Here I should add that, from my own experience of telepathic pain, there appears to be some kind of physical-to-physical psi as well. This doesn't seem to be covered in the literature so far.

Carroll B. Nash, a biologist turned parapsychologist, is one of the few to summarise and enumerate the properties of psi.[5] The most intriguing of these is the fact that psi is unlimited by space or time. It doesn't weaken over large distances and appears to be instantaneous, regardless of the distance between the 'transmitter' and the recipient. Moreover, it operates even when the experimenters are in metal chambers, Faraday cages and in caves deep below ground. This implies that it isn't an electro-magnetic force, as it doesn't work like radio waves following the curvature of the earth. It is also not blocked by intervening material bodies or fields.

Whatever psi is, Jessica Utts, a statistics professor at UC Irvine, believes there is more than enough evidence that it exists. In 1999 she published a study entitled *The Significance of Statistics in Mind-Matter Research*. She compared the strength of the results of parapsychological experiments with those establishing, for example, that a daily dose of aspirin helps

---

5.   Nash (1986) p.213 quoted in Beichler (2017)

prevent a heart attack, showing that the evidence for psi is stronger than for the effectiveness of popular pharmaceutical drugs. In spite of this, the scientific community continues to ignore this phenomenon.

Thomas Etter of the Boundary Institute, a non-profit scientific research centre in Los Altos, California, focussing on the development and exploration of physics, quantum theories of physics, mathematics and their linked relationships, has made the following comment: 'When a belief is widely held in the face of overwhelming evidence to the contrary, we call it a superstition. By that criterion, the most egregious superstition of modern times, perhaps of all time, is the 'scientific' belief in the non-existence of psi.'[6]

Edward Lorenz presented a famous paper in 1972 at the American Association for the Advancement of Science entitled *'Predictability: Does the Flap of a Butterfly's Wings in Brazil set off a Tornado in Texas?'*. This gave rise to the idea of the 'butterfly effect', whereby everything in our world is interconnected.

Brian Josephson, professor of physics at Cambridge University and 1973 Nobel Laureate for his work on quantum tunnelling, said of Radin's book *The Conscious Universe*: 'Cutting perceptively through the spurious arguments frequently made by sceptics, [Radin] shows that the evidence in favour of [paranormal] existence is overwhelming.'[7]

But is psi the same as consciousness, or the soul? For Richards, it is the daemon, 'the higher part of ourselves – that part of the self which inspires us, which manifests ESP and intuition, and which passes forth from the body during astral

6. Radin (2006) p.35 introductory quote to Chapter 3
7. Radin (2006) endorsement

projection, while the soul remains behind.'[8] For the paraphysicist Beichler, 'psychic' or paranormal abilities are part of a sixth sense, not the same as consciousness (connectivity to the five-dimensional single field).

However, what stands out from the occurrences Dragana and I have experienced is the extraordinary circumstances surrounding them, those of imminent death and great pain. These seem to heighten and facilitate extra-sensory perception when there is no other form of communication available.

There is also evidence that people use telepathy when hypnotised. This was reported nearly 200 years ago by Puységur in his *Memoirs in Aid of a History of Animal Magnetism*, where under hypnosis he would give mental orders to his subject, Victor, who would carry them out as if they had been spoken. He could also get Victor to repeat the words of a song Puységur was singing mentally, not out loud. Interestingly enough, it was noted that Victor, who was not a young man of great intelligence, became much more intelligent and perceptive when hypnotised.

In 2014 one hundred scientists, including twenty Nobel Prize winners, made a call in *Frontiers in Human Neuroscience* (2014; 8:17) for an open, informed study of all aspects of consciousness. They differed in the extent to which they were convinced that the case for psi phenomena has already been made, but not in their view of science as a non-dogmatic, open, critical but respectful process that requires thorough consideration of all evidence, as well as scepticism toward both the assumptions they already hold and those that challenge them.

---

8.   Richards (2015) p.119. See also p.19 of this book for a fuller explanation.

What is clear is that normal scientific method is of little use when trying to explain telepathy. Yet Dragana and I know it happens and would like some explanation. Is it so unbelievable that mammals, at least, may have some form of extra-sensory communication they can use, especially at times of crisis? Was it perhaps used by early humans before they had speech? Is it related to some form of instinct?

It certainly seems extremely odd that we, 'the highest' of the animals, should be thought to lack any phenomenal powers whilst we recognise them in so many other animals. Just think of dogs and their anticipation of their owners' return home. 'Videotaped experiments carried out under controlled conditions showed that the dogs' anticipations of their owners' returns did not depend on routine times of return, or on clues from the people at home, or on sounds from familiar cars, or on any other sensory clues. They appeared to depend on their owners' intentions at a distance, and were essentially telepathic.'[9]

Willis Harman, president of the Institute of Noetic Sciences from 1977 to 1997 said 'Perhaps the only limits to the human mind are those we believe in.'

These are questions I would love to hear scientists discuss, taking on trust the word of countless people who have had telepathic experiences, instead of insisting that nothing is proven unless their scientific method of repeatability and predictability is used.

---

9.   Sheldrake (2004) p. 85

4.

Me in two places at once: 1972

Bilocation, quantum superposition, ghosts of the living

If at first the idea is not absurd, then there is no hope for it.
ALBERT EINSTEIN

In the end, I enjoyed teaching English in Finland. The saying went that the Finns took about three months to decide whether they liked you or not. If they did, they would start answering your questions with more than a monosyllable. I must have met with their approval – they became quite chatty in the Finnish sense of the word by Christmas time. By the time of the midnight sun (well, almost – it would get dark around 11pm and then light again at 1am where I was in the south of the country), the flow of conversation was sometimes kept up for a good ten minutes at a time.

I had found my vocation in life. What better job was there than teaching your native tongue? You knew when anyone was making a mistake and you knew what the correct version was. You were going to need a bit of jargon to back this up, but basically you had the makings of success before you even started. I made enquiries at the British Council and discovered that I could do a teaching degree in Teaching English as a Foreign Language (TEFL). I also found myself a job teaching on a summer school in Folkestone through a contact at the Council. So, waving goodbye to my new-found friends, I prepared myself for my new career.

When I think of Folkestone, I think of expanses of fine lawn, colourful flower borders and all that is best of summers in England. (Yes, you've guessed it – the sun really did shine every day but it was never too hot.) I liked The School of English Studies, Peter O'Connell, the Principal, and Folkestone straight away. That summer school was a great learning experience, with colleagues passing on tips about activities and games that worked with the mainly teenage students, giving them a fun way to learn English. And there was a marvellous garden for tea parties and a spacious flat to stay in with high ceilings and big sash windows. Teachers accompanied students on all kinds of trips and visits as part of the course, and there was a social on Friday nights with music and dancing.

It was towards the end of the summer when, on the last Friday evening of the course before the compulsory social, I walked down to the cliff overlooking the sea in front of the Grand Hotel with Hilary, one of the other teachers I'd got friendly with. It was one of those calm, warm endings to a perfect summer's day when you feel fulfilled and content. The French coast opposite was so clear in every detail it looked close enough to row there in half an hour.

France! Such a longing came over me. I turned to Hilary and told her how much I'd like to just jump on the ferry and go across the Channel, have a simple meal of crusty baguette with Camembert and some red wine. I told her about my time in Bordeaux. We Bristol students had spent a semester at Bordeaux University in our second year. Our French lectrice at Bristol, Françoise Perrotin, had asked her father, the Professor of French Literature at Bordeaux, to take me on a tour of the famous vineyards. To this day, a sip of St Emilion never fails to take me back to that languid June day of degustational pampering and amiable conversation. I told Hilary all about my yearning for the life of quiet pleasure I had tasted in France, until she looked at her watch and we realised we had five minutes to get back to the School for the social.

It was a pleasant evening. We had a nondescript Saturday – an English afternoon tea to reinforce the students' ideas about our strange customs and a trip to the funfair. Sunday morning found all of the teachers on the summer school in the staff room to say goodbye to each other. Jim came into the room and hurried over to where I was sitting. I hardly knew him – we had not been teaching similar age groups or together supervising trips, so we had only ever seen each other across the staff room and said 'Hello' when we passed in the corridor.

'How was France?' he asked with a smile.

'Sorry?' I replied in confusion.

'Your trip to France. You know, my brother met you on the ferry on Friday night.'

'Oh no,' I said with a smile. 'It must have been someone else he met. I haven't been to France this weekend.'

'Well, there isn't any other Pat teaching on this summer school, is there? Anyway, he described you minutely. It couldn't have been anyone else.'

I felt cold for a moment and completely nonplussed. But then I laughed.

'Come on, Jim,' I said. 'It's not very funny. Stop kidding.'

But Jim looked incredulous and indignant.

'Why are you trying to pretend you weren't on the ferry with my brother?' he asked in a hurt tone.

Now it was my turn to be indignant.

'I'm not pretending,' I replied. 'I wasn't on it. Ask anyone. They can tell you I was at the social on Friday night and then at the afternoon tea and the funfair last night. I've been here all the time, haven't I, Hilary?'

By this time, not just Hilary was listening to our conversation.

'Do you remember, on Friday evening you were saying…' she began.

'Yes, exactly,' I interrupted. 'That's what worries me. I was only saying, just before the dance, how marvellous it'd be to go to France – there and then. Drop everything and *go*! How I'd love to be in France and that kind of thing… This all seems horribly uncanny. You're not joking, Jim? 'Cos if you are, you're a fantastic actor!'

But Jim had gone very pale.

'How strange!' he said after a pause. 'But Joe described you exactly – couldn't have been anyone else – I mean, you're not exactly common or usual-looking…'

'Thank you, I think,' I replied.

'No, but, well, anyway, there aren't any other Pats and this is the only summer school…'

Peter O'Connell came in and started talking to us. We all stood staring at each other for another few moments and then turned to look at Peter. We were telling ourselves there must be some explanation…

Now, of course, I wish I'd insisted on meeting Jim's brother, but at the time I didn't want to think about the implications of what had happened.

చా

This experience in Folkestone is, without a doubt, the one I wish I could dismiss with some simple explanation. It happened exactly as I have recounted because I wrote it all down that day so I wouldn't forget. It came back to me forcefully, however, one day recently when I was watching a programme about quantum mechanics.

The presenter was explaining quantum superposition. This principle suggests that particles can exist in two separate locations at once. Quantum superposition is made even more perplexing by the fact that it can only occur when the particles are unobserved. Simply by observing a particle in two different quantum states, you cause what is known as 'wave function collapse', and the particle again exists in only one state or the other (and in the case of superposition, only one physical location or the other). Therefore, measuring a particle in superposition is incredibly difficult. The whole thing is not only 'spooky' as Einstein called it, but is really quite impossible to grasp for our human brains. Dr Andrew Powell puts it well: 'There is no such thing as reality that stands apart from the observer.'[10]

What physicists tell us happens to these particles is, of course, what happened to me. I existed in two separate locations at once. Who knows how often this might happen in life? If we don't meet anyone we know, or a person we meet never comments on the fact, we won't be aware of having been in two places at once. I only know it happened to me that summer of 1972 because someone else reported back on me being somewhere where I wasn't, to my knowledge.

---

10.   Powell p.136

The Roman Catholic Church recognises several examples of pious men who could be in two places at once. One such was St Francis Xavier, who founded the Jesuit Order in the 16th century: he regularly performed missionary work in two locations many miles apart at the same time. Another was Padre Pio, an Italian Capuchin priest living in the 20th century, who was claimed to have bi-located on many occasions within his native country and abroad.

A fascination with the idea of being able to be in two places at once is exploited in Stephen King's novel *The Outsider*, where there is watertight evidence that a man accused of murder was physically present at the scene, but also 70 miles away, where there is video of him, as well as his fingerprints and a number of eyewitnesses. In *The Last Jedi*, the eighth instalment of the *Star Wars* saga, Luke Skywalker is simultaneously fighting on one planet whilst meditating on another.

It is, of course, shamanic practice to travel with part of the soul. The word *shaman* comes from the Tungusic languages of North Asia, but very similar shamanic practice has been reported all over the world in a wide variety of cultures. It involves reaching an altered state of consciousness, perceived as part of the soul 'travelling', during which the shaman can interact with the spirit world and achieve healing and release of trauma.

Some anthropologists think shamanism is actually a surviving ancient Paleolithic religion. It seems, however, that shamanic journeys are not interpreted as actual physical journeys of part of the practitioner but often involve experiencing an animal's life, running as a deer or flying as a bird. They are thus rather different from a person being in two places at once in the same form.

My experience could be interpreted as that of 'a ghost of the living'. 'Ghosts of the Living' are one of the eight types of ghosts set up by ghost hunter Peter Underwood, quoted in Roger Clarke's *A Natural History of Ghosts : 500 Years of Hunting for Proof*. The author believes this type is one of the greatest discoveries of The Society for Psychical Research, which published two volumes with 701 case studies in 1886 under the title *Phantasms of the Living*.

Perhaps the most impressive case Clarke cites is the one of a man who had moved house from Robertsbridge in Sussex. The family who had bought his house came to visit him in his new cottage several years later. When he opened the door to greet them, the daughter fainted. On regaining consciousness, she explained that she had seen him many times in the garden of his old house.

Clarke sees ghosts of the living as suggesting 'something of the brain function behind certain paranormal phenomena and indicate that such phenomena are actually nothing to do with the dead at all. Somehow, using ESP and the ability of the brain to generate images, some invisible signal is accessed and processed.' (But I was clearly very much a normal physical presence on the ferry, not a ghostly apparition.)

Actually, this relates back to the 'ghosts' I described in the first chapter – the ginger kitten and the elderly woman in the A&E department. Perhaps it is another illustration of the two bodies we are said to have: the carbon-based one and the bioplasma one. If this theory is correct, it implies that strong emotion, such as my longing to be in France, can trigger the separation of the two bodies, not just the experience of death.

5.

The Folkestone fortune teller: 1973

Clairvoyance, reincarnation and predestination

But what do I know of Time itself – Time that must be a point before it extends into a line, the conceptual Time in stillness before it becomes perpetual time in motion?

V.DWARAKNATH REDDY,
THE PHYSICS OF KARMA: A REQUIEM TO TIME

I went back to Folkestone the following year to teach English on the summer school again. Jim wasn't there, so the weird incident of me being in two places at once was further buried in my memory.

The intervening year had been spent at The University College of North Wales, Bangor, doing that Dip.Ed. course in TEFL. I was looking forward to being back in Folkestone for the summer school. This time I was to share a flat next to the School of English Studies with Noelle, a woman in her forties from New Zealand, who was currently teaching in Spain. She had dark brown wavy hair and a kind of feline posture – you felt she might pounce at any moment. Her most striking feature was her eyes, which were dark brown and had a startling intensity to them.

Noelle took me under her wing and made me her acolyte. She was searching for Mr Right and had recently visited a clairvoyant in Folkestone, who had impressed her with a vision of how she was going to meet a good-looking middle-aged man with a brown jacket, a sleek Dalmatian dog in tow. A few days after this consultation, Noelle met the very man walking the dog on the cliffs, and she was now going out with him.

'That woman is truly psychic,' she panted huskily. That was Noelle's usual way of speaking. Everything was uttered with a kind of excited breathiness.

I had made the mistake of opening myself up to Noelle over one of the dinners she had cooked for us (she was a good cook and wine always accompanied the food). I had told her I didn't know where my life was going and I was more than a little lost.

'What you need is to go and see Edna Stocker,' she declared. Edna Stocker was the clairvoyant. 'She'll sort you out. She'll tell you where your future lies.'

So, one fateful evening, there I was in front of a nondescript semi-detached house in an unprepossessing part of the town, standing outside the gate and wondering if it really was a good idea to let Edna Stocker sort me out. I had an appointment at 7pm. It was five past. I took a deep breath and headed down the path to the front door. I rang the bell and Edna Stocker opened the door after a short pause. She looked like a very ordinary housewife in her fifties, dressed in a drab blouse and skirt, and she talked like a kindly aunt.

'Come in, dear – Pat, isn't it? This way. We'll sit in the front room.'

The furniture was typical of the day, no exotic screens, Turkish rugs or dramatic curtains; a bulky, rather ugly, green three-piece suite, a Sixties modernistic-looking gas fire, a drop-leaf table with two chairs round it, varnished in a dark tint hiding the grain of the wood. Edna pointed to one of the chairs and invited me to sit down. She took the other chair. Without more ado, she handed me the pack of playing cards on the table and asked me to shuffle them and choose seven, which I was to hand to her, face down. I did as I was told.

Edna laid the cards out on the table, face up, and started talking in a conversational manner, nothing of the gypsy fortune teller about it. She might have been discussing the weather.

'You're going to get fed up with teaching kids,' she said, focussing on one of the playing cards. All right, Noelle might have phoned her and told her I was a fellow teacher on the summer school.

'You'll do another course, more exams, letters after your name. You'll always go on learning.' I'd just done exams, finished my Dip Ed – I wasn't too keen on the idea of more studying.

'You'll always move in intellectual circles,' Edna continued. 'Your husband will be four or five years older than you. He's tall, lean, very dark. His hair is receding at the sides, it's curly. He'll be a dominating man. Very brilliant. A professor? Teaching students? Connected with the UN? I really can't quite say what he does for a living. You'll do a lot of travel together and live in an old house with a rambling garden in the country. There are ruins, olive groves, a hot climate. Maybe Israel, or Greece.

'Three children I can see – two boys and a tomboy daughter,' Edna went on, her eyes on another card now. 'You'll live near the sea, do a lot of swimming. Your house will be very happy, untidy. Your husband and you are generally very casual, but you both dress up very well and smartly for occasions when he gives talks and things like that. You'll have lots of dinner parties.'

Edna paused. 'You have an emerald and diamond antique

engagement ring which you don't wear often. Lots of pottery and hessian in your house. You both have jobs. You're teaching adults. You'll never want for anything.'

There was another pause. Edna seemed to be running out of things to say.

'You'll always be in love,' she suddenly added. 'Married for more than forty years.

'Three grey hairs,' she declared. 'you'll have three grey hairs growing from your crown and you won't be able to pluck them out always. Very annoying.

'Your table will have lots of bottles on it, lots of salads, almost vegetarian,' Edna continued, her eyes on another card. 'There's a man you love. I don't know if you've already met him or not. You'll always have a pure and beautiful relationship with him, but you'll do much better than him. There'll always be great affection between you, like a brother and sister…

'Your children might be in school in England,' she finally announced. Then she looked straight at me, taking her eyes off the cards. 'Never go to Canada,' she added abruptly. 'Don't ask me why. Just don't go. That's all I see. I can't see further than forty years ahead.'

She had said a lot for me to take in and I was fascinated how she worked. It was clear she wasn't making things up at random.

'Why did you ask me to choose cards?' I asked.

'I focus on them and see pictures, scenes from your life,' Edna explained simply.

The session was over. I paid Edna the sum agreed (it wasn't exorbitant) and left.

My first year of teaching with a proper qualification wasn't abroad. I decided to teach kids coming to the UK and needing to learn English. I found a post at William Morris Senior High School in Walthamstow, North London. The School had a group of Ugandan Asian pupils, who had been thrown out of the country with their families by the dictator, Idi Amin.

My group of fourteen-year-old Asians who had turned up in Walthamstow were courteous and middle-class, but their English was pretty rudimentary. When asked what they would like to do when they left school, they invariably said 'Me engineer' or 'Me doctor' – the five boys, that is. The three girls said very little and required written exercises to do in a huddle in the corner of the classroom while the boys held centre stage. My objections to this gender inequality were met with incomprehension by all concerned, and in the end, I had to agree to the arrangement, which was condoned by the Head of Department.

Over the following year, I gained true affection for my Asian boys and became very protective of them. It was only when I discussed them with other staff that I realised how unrealistic their dreams of professional careers were. The general opinion was that they were all doomed to unskilled manual labour even if they did learn passable English. I began to find it all depressing and I was getting itchy feet again.

I started applying for posts for English language teachers at universities in the Soviet Union and Yugoslavia, recruited by the British Council. I wanted to see how communism worked, a fascination at the time. My interview for the Soviet Union came first and I withdrew my application after hearing I would have no freedom whatsoever about what I taught and how I taught it. Everything would have to be literally 'textbook'.

Yugoslavia was a different matter. The chair of the

interviewing panel was a different man from the Soviet interviews. When one of the panel asked me why I wanted to go to Yugoslavia, he jumped in before I had a chance to say anything with the observation:

'Well, she's got Slavic cheekbones!'

This was a revelation to me. It was the first indication that I might be going to a country where I would fit in, as opposed to my country of birth, where everyone took me for a foreigner. My Mum had a snub nose and my Dad olive skin and the combination in me made me look distinctly un-English, though no one was ever quite sure where to place my origins. Now, finally, someone had said I had a salient Slavic feature.

A few days later I was offered the post at the University of Skopje in the Yugoslav Republic of Macedonia, in the south of the country, next to Greece. Having said a regretful goodbye to my students and with *Teach Yourself Serbo-Croat* in hand, I set off for my new job.

I was met at Skopje railway station by quite a delegation from the English Department. One of them took it on himself to give me a guided tour of the city and introduce me to other recent graduates my age. He was a jolly but shy young man with deep brown eyes and receding hair, but he was not the man I was fated to marry. I didn't recognise the man Edna had described to me.

I wasn't given much chance to be lonely as I had been in Finland. I often met up with my new colleagues and went to see a Russian production of Molière's *Don Juan* with them. We had tickets upstairs. Just before the production started, they pointed to a man coming in downstairs with a woman and going to sit on the front row in the stalls.

It was him – the man Edna had described. How I knew, seeing him from that distance, I have no idea, but a tremendous thrill went through me that I had seen the man who was to be my husband. I was told his name was Goran and he was to come to the Department as an Assistant Lecturer in English Literature. Strange to say, I relaxed and enjoyed the production. I knew I would meet Goran sooner or later and I was in no hurry. There was just a settled conviction that all would turn out as it should and I could put myself in the hands of Fate.

It was a few weeks later when we finally met. My colleagues and I had had another lunch with plenty of beer and all felt the urge to sing English songs. 'We'll go and get a guitar,' someone said, and off we drove to a street in the new part of town. They knocked on a door and who should answer but Goran. My heart jumped. He went back into the house and emerged with a guitar in his hand. He took his place on the back seat next to me. We chatted and it soon emerged that his English was just about perfect.

We went back to my flat and sang all the songs we could think of. Goran says to this day that he seduced me with The Incredible String Band's *My Name is Death*. I loved its medieval tonality and sentiment:

> My name is Death, cannot you see?
> All life must turn to me.
> Oh, cannot you see?
> And you must come with me,
> You must come with me.

There really is no saying what's going to make you fall in love with someone. Like many young people, I was attracted to

Gothic romanticism and, of course, still under the influence of the French Middle Ages and courtly troubadours. Goran thought that song did the trick. He was wrong. I had already known he was the man for me that evening I saw him at the theatre. Could he have done anything to put me off? Had Edna not told me I was going to marry him, would I have given him a second glance? Would we have stayed together from that day on?

We met on 22nd October 1974 and have been together ever since. We started living together in my flat. I got to know his family and was accepted by them.

Goran and I were married on 14th March 1976. My parents couldn't come for the wedding, as Mum was not allowed to fly. She had angina and had had a heart attack during the operation for her second hip replacement, that time she broke her pelvis in a fall in the hospital and I felt the pain out in Finland. But Mum and Dad arranged a wedding blessing in the local village church for when we were in England during the summer holidays.

Everyone was impressed with Goran's bridegroom speech at the reception. Not only did he speak such good English but he also made jokes, like inviting them all to come and visit us in Skopje – but not all at once. The photos show the yellow grass everywhere outside the church and hotel, and even in our garden, which was, as always, kept perfect by Dad with his green fingers. He had to use the washing-up water to water the garden as there was a hosepipe ban because of the tropical temperatures and the lack of rain. The summer of 1976 went down in history as the hottest summer on record and I don't think even the summer of 2018 has surpassed it.

❧

A lot of what Edna said was to turn out to be true, but quite a few details did not. I think the clue to why this was so is in the fact that Edna said she focussed on the cards to see pictures of my life. I have never yet lived by the sea in a large house with lots of pottery and hessian, but I have stayed in many houses like that and have spent time in hot countries by the sea almost every year. The engagement ring Edna saw was my mother's sapphire and diamond one, which I rarely wear. I suppose it's hard to distinguish between sapphires and emeralds when you get a quick flash of a scene in someone's life.

It seems certain people can see pictures of the future or the past if given objects belonging to someone, or with their imprint. There are famous incidents of crimes being solved in this way. Again, we come back to the idea of people imprinting things with their own radiation or energy, and the notion of another plane unconnected with linear time. The disquieting implication, of course, is that our lives are already mapped out.

When considering what happened when Auntie Dorothy dreamt about an event that was to take place only six months later, I looked at the concept of Time and the idea that we can somehow step out of the 'timeline' of our lives and fast forward to the future. Something like this must surely be occurring with clairvoyance.

Gordon Smith, among Britain's most respected mediums, has addressed this issue in his book *One Hundred Answers from Spirit: Britain's Greatest Medium Answers the Great Questions of Life and Death*. His answer on this is within the context of his assertion that our consciousness is reincarnated. This can happen in a second or after thousands of years – there is no fixed time span. For each reincarnation, parents are chosen at a much higher level of consciousness between all involved in the future journey, the relationships and interactions which the travelling consciousness needs to experience. According to Smith, 'the waiting consciousness fuses or bonds with the chemicals of two mating adults, so the spirit is in the foetus from conception. Consciousness is ever acting, moving and changing. Each spirit is just a minute component of the vastness of consciousness.'

Although many of us will associate belief in reincarnation with Indian religions such as Buddhism, Jainism, Hinduism and Sikhism, it was held by Ancient Greek philosophers like Pythagoras, Socrates and Plato and is found in a number of tribal societies all over the world in places as far apart as Siberia and Australia. Certain heretical Christian groups like the Cathars and Bogomils have also believed in reincarnation. The feeling that a humanist or atheist like me may have that the aim of life is to improve ourselves, to become the best person we can be, is perhaps related to this, the final point of reincarnation in the Indian religions being *moksha*, or *nirvana*, liberation from this cycle of birth and rebirth when true self-knowledge and self-perfection have been achieved in a state of bliss. During each life, the soul will have a task related to this ultimate aim.

However, this theory implies predestination: the course of our lives is already determined and we have no free will. This is one of the key paradoxes of Christianity, of course: if all events are willed by God, how can human beings also have free will? Smith, the medium quoted above, claims that we have free will 'within this structure of predestiny'. In other words, we give ourselves options, like different paths we can take. At a turning point in our lives, we direct ourselves onto a particular path or what can be called a 'timeline'; it will have a different outcome from if we had chosen an alternative path.

Predestination is clearly a thorny issue but proof of reincarnation is impressive. Beichler[11] developed Past-Life Regression (PLR). It involves hypnotising a person to remember events of a previous life or lives, and ties up with the belief that some psychological and medical problems are holdovers from previous lives and can only be treated when their source is known. He references Dr Ian Stevenson, a psychiatrist at the University of Virginia, who investigated hundreds of fully-documented cases of children with spontaneous past-life memories.

Stevenson also studied deformities, anomalies and birthmarks which could not be attributed to either heredity or occurrences at birth, and had spectacular results. One memorable case was of a boy born with a mottled scar on his chest who remembered his former name and being killed by a shotgun blast to the chest. When verified, this turned out to relate to a man who had really existed and suffered this fate.

Stevenson also examined phobias in cases where previous deaths had been caused under special circumstances (eg fear of water in the case of drowning), likes and dislikes associated with previous lives, continuity of habits manifesting at an early age (alcoholism, drug-taking, etc), special abilities and talents carried over into a new life. Sometimes even a knowledge of a foreign language is transferred.

I will come back to Edna Stocker's visions of my life for the next forty years and how correct she was in following chapters.

---

11.   Beichler, James E. (2008)

6.

Take me to South America: 1980
Inception and entanglement

The following year Goran had to go off and do his national service in the Yugoslav army. He was stationed in Raška, a Serbian town reached from Skopje by crossing Kosovo. I would go and visit him every fortnight driving the 2CV6 we had bought together before we were even married.

The army took its toll on Goran. He was seriously depressed when he came out in 1978 and had claustrophobia after travelling in a closed army truck for several hours, packed in like sardines with other conscripts. He seemed to be living in his own nightmare world where I couldn't reach him. I had to fly home to the UK that summer to see my family and friends alone.

Dad greeted me with the news that Mum had had a second heart attack and was in the local cottage hospital in Melton Mowbray. I managed to see her before she had her third, fatal heart attack in that hospital. It took me three years before I could talk about her without tears.

Over the next six months after I returned to Skopje, Goran gradually recovered from his period of depression. Having completed an MA in Belgrade on the theatre of Samuel Beckett, he became keen to do more postgraduate study: a PhD on the theatre of Edward Bond, combining his love of theatre with his academic career at the University. He applied for a British Council scholarship to spend a year researching in the UK. He was duly awarded the scholarship and together we looked at various British universities known for their Drama and Linguistics Departments. I had decided that I would take the opportunity of doing an MA in Linguistics while he did his PhD research. (Edna was to be proved right about those letters after my name.) We settled on Manchester.

In September 1979 we arrived in that great northern city after a three-day drive across Western Europe and moved into the first-floor flat in Didsbury owned by Mr Vickers downstairs. He was a delightful man with a great sense of humour. He called our 2CV6 'The Iron Lung' and the neighbour across the road, who spent hours washing and polishing his car every Sunday, 'Mr Happy Motoring'.

Not long after we'd arrived, I had my thirtieth birthday, which occasioned an unexpected triggering of my biological clock.

'Goran, I want a baby,' I declared, against all logic and convenience, since I was at the beginning of a one-year MA course, to be followed by the writing of a dissertation over another year in order to be awarded my degree. But having a baby became my obsession and, being a methodical and thorough sort of person, I studied how to get pregnant (my daughter tells me there's an app for this nowadays – of course).

At Easter Goran flew to Belgrade to attend the Yugoslav Theatre Festival in Novi Sad. His second play – and the one which would turn out to be the most famous of all, now on the Macedonian school curriculum – swept the board of prizes with the Skopje Dramski Teatar production directed by his friend, Slobodan Unkovski.

Being impecunious at the time, I stayed in the UK and went to see my friend Ceri back in North Wales, near Bangor, where

I had done my teaching degree. Ceri was amazed at how many eggs and pieces of bacon I would down for breakfast every day. I did a pregnancy test and discovered Goran and I had hit the jackpot – it was positive.

On 8th May that year we sat in front of Mr Vickers's TV watching President Tito's funeral. Tito had kept Yugoslavia together and non-aligned as a socialist country for nearly thirty-five years. Little did we foresee that day that in just over a decade the state he helped to found would no longer exist.

We returned to Skopje in the summer, having both achieved our goals: meeting Edward Bond and studying his plays for Goran, and passing my MA exams for me. Some of the summer holiday was spent down by Lake Ohrid, one of the oldest and deepest lakes in the world with its own very special pink trout. The only bad experience I had there was a nasty stomach bug from swimming in the lake. A friend cured it with the bitterest tea I've ever tasted – pomegranate.

Our baby was due on 1st December and I had, of course, read all the right books, done the right exercises, applied the right cream to avoid stretch marks and practised the breathing and panting when in labour. However, ten days went by before I had any pains. I was taken into hospital, where the pains promptly ceased. I was put on a heart monitor for the baby and left alone. The beep of the heart beat suddenly stopped. Just as I was about to scream for a nurse, it started again, only to stop a few beeps later. This went on for twenty minutes before a nurse finally came to check on me. She told me there was nothing to worry about – the machine was probably faulty – but my gynaecologist turned up and decided to do an emergency Caesarean.

I was quickly prepared for the operation and wheeled into the freezing operating theatre. When they saw my teeth chattering, they turned on a two-bar electric heater high up on the wall. It was the last thing I remember seeing before I went under the anaesthetic. Then I found myself up near the heater looking down on myself covered in the green sheet. I didn't think much about that at the time, but I was to remember it years later.

The next thing I knew, a thrilled-looking Goran was leaning over me saying:

'Patty, we've got a little boy!'

All I managed was an unenthusiastic 'Oh.' It was as if I was underwater, hearing only a distorted voice. I stayed in hospital for three weeks. I had an infection which they didn't seem able to cure with any of the different antibiotics they injected into me.

Every day they would bring me my baby son. My milk didn't come properly, so most days we would just sit there looking at each other. He didn't cry – they must have fed him well with formula before he arrived.

To understand what I said to my baby on one of those days you need some background. For many years I had been fascinated by Central and South America. Before I met Goran, a job teaching English in Latin America had been next on the wish list after perhaps five years in Yugoslavia. I don't know when that interest started or where it came from, but it has always been strong in my life. Teaching English in Latin America was obviously now unlikely, but the fascination remained – I had recently been reading *The Ancient Sun Kingdoms of the Americas*. One day in hospital, looking down at my – as yet nameless

– son cradled in my arms, I told him:

'When you grow up, you're going to take me to South America.'

I don't remember explicitly saying anything else to him during those three weeks, except singing to him very softly so no one else would hear on the packed ward.

Having plied me with any number of antibiotics which didn't work, the doctors finally decided to do a hysterectomy. The nurses prepared me for the operation but no one thought to tell me what was going on. Luckily, my father-in-law had a cousin who was a specialist in gastroenterology and he came to ask if he could x-ray my intestines before they operated on me. I was wheeled over to his department and, sure enough, the x-ray showed I had peritonitis – my digestive system had stopped working. After the right treatment, I came out of the hospital with womb intact. It was already New Year's Eve.

The long discussions went on about what to call our son. Goran and I both liked the Macedonian equivalents of John and Andrew, but they were written Jane and Andrea, so not really ideal for a boy who was half-English. It was Goran's father who came up with the name Igor, which everyone liked and I accepted on condition I could call him Iggy. None of us being aficionados of the horror film genre, we didn't know that Igor was the name of a stock character in such films, assistant to Dr Frankenstein or Dracula. This fact only emerged when Igor was at grammar school in England years later.

At the age of seventeen, Iggy was asking to be called Ig rather than the more childish nickname he had had since birth. It reminded me of my telling my father I was henceforth to be called Pat rather than Patsy. Ig was in his final year at school and thinking about his future. He was lukewarm about going to university and didn't know what he would want to study.

One day Goran sat him down with the UCLES catalogue and went through the courses open to him. He was studying English, Spanish and History for A Level. After a distinct lack of enthusiasm for everything Goran suggested, they alighted upon a course at King's College, London: United States and Latin American Studies. When I was shown the details, it didn't take me long to work out what Ig found attractive about it – the third year was spent half at the University of California, Santa Cruz, and half at the University of Mérida, Mexico.

I can't remember now when it struck me that he was going to fulfil the prediction I had made in hospital as he lay in my arms a couple of weeks old. Prediction is the wrong word. I had simply told him he was going to take me to South America. Sure enough, when he was in Mexico in 2003, I joined him for a three-week holiday and he did indeed take me around. I had very rudimentary Spanish from some adult education classes I'd taken, but Ig endeared himself to everyone on the continent with his fluent Latin American Spanish. We spent a week in Mexico, mainly in Mexico City, a week in Peru and a week in Bolivia, where Pete, my friend from Walthamstow, had then retired and was running a restaurant, three hours by bus from La Paz.

That trip to Latin America was one of the highlights of my life. I shall never forget sitting on a stone wall looking down over Machu Picchu, the tears streaming down my face. I don't know why I was so moved but I was certainly overjoyed that my son had made my dream come true.

Interestingly enough, when Ig graduated, he had no desire to pursue a career teaching Spanish or connected with Latin America. He quickly became engrossed in trying to be of use to the country where he was born, his fatherland of Macedonia. He did an MA in Advanced European and International Studies at the European Institute, followed by a short internship with the EU Information Centre in Skopje, going on to live in the city of his birth for a few years. But his experience was the same as many young men and women who had gone abroad to study and come back to be of use to their homeland – he didn't find a job where he could apply his knowledge.

Some years later he did another MA in Interpreting at Skopje University and again wrote a fine dissertation on the cultural problems involved, but by then he had got married to Plamena, who worked for the EU Commission and was posted away from Brussels, where Ig could have used his new degree, to Tirana, where it was of little use as he didn't speak Albanian.

Ig, Plamena, their nearly three-year-old daughter Kalina and I were to go on a memorable trip to the Yucatan in Mexico in December 2015 to see the Mayan monuments Ig and I hadn't seen in 2003. Ig's wonderful Latin American Spanish was again a great asset. However, that was just a great holiday. My son's undergraduate studies had led to nothing in terms of the course of his life and work after graduation.

It really did seem as if he had fulfilled the task I had assigned him to do as a two-week-old baby in taking me to South America and had then got on with the life he had really wanted to lead.

℘

It seems you can subconsciously implant an idea in a person's mind, even as a baby, which they feel compelled to carry out. In science fiction, the term *inception* has been introduced to refer to the act of instilling an idea into someone's mind by entering his or her dreams. The film *Inception* is the most famous example of this. It is the story of a professional thief, played by Leonardo di Caprio, who penetrates a victim's subconscious to steal information. He takes the opportunity offered to him of erasing his own criminal history by implanting an idea into a target's subconscious.

It seems we are back to quantum physics here in trying to explain how this is possible. With the psychologist Carl Jung, Nobel Laureate quantum physicist Wolfgang Pauli developed the idea of *unus mundus*, one unified reality from which everything originates and to which it returns. This relates to Jung's famous concept of synchronicity, whereby an observer and a connected phenomenon come together in a 'meaningful coincidence' in that they stem from the same source.[12] The link with quantum mechanics is clear: particles are not separate entities but related throughout space and time in a way which Einstein referred to as 'spooky action at a distance'. Austrian physicist Erwin Schrödinger, he of the alive-and-dead cat fame, called this relationship 'entanglement'.

The concept of the interconnectedness of everything is, of course, central to Buddhism and Hinduism. We are perhaps less aware that it was a tenet of Ancient Greek philosophers before Socrates,[13] and came down to Aristotle. It seems scientists are finally coming round to a view of reality which coincides with

---

12. I come back to synchronicity and Jung's best-known case of it leading to a breakthrough in the treatment of his patient on p.85.

13. Zatta, Claudia (2017)

ancient philosophical beliefs.

Parapsychologist Dean Radin has not unreasonably applied the idea of entanglement to our minds,[14] continuing Jung's work. He writes:

'Science is at the very earliest stages of understanding entanglement, and there is much yet to learn. But what we've seen so far provides a new way of thinking about psi. No longer are psi experiences regarded as rare human talents, divine gifts, or 'powers' that magically transcend ordinary physical boundaries. Instead, psi becomes an unavoidable consequence of living in an interconnected, entangled physical reality. Psi is reframed from a bizarre anomaly that doesn't fit into the normal world - and hence labeled paranormal - into a natural phenomenon of physics.'

My own experience of inception could well be described as an experience of psi, a real entanglement of minds between me and my son. But some might say it was a prophecy, that I was seeing the future. According to parapsychologists, it seems inception and prophecy would both be included in the concept of psi, whether it involves entanglement or stepping outside the 'timeline', all part of 'the block universe' mentioned in Chapter 2. I'll come back to this again in Chapter 11 when looking at cases of premonition or precognition.

14.   Radin, Dean (2006)

7

You nearly died when you were thirty: 1989/1980

Palmistry and Near-Death Experiences

It is a stupid presumption to go about despising and condemning as false anything that seems to us improbable; this is a common fault among those who think they have more intelligence than the crowd. I used to be like that once, and if I heard talk of ghosts walking or prognostications of future events, of enchantments or sorceries, or some other tale I could not swallow, I would pity the poor people who were taken in by such nonsense. And now I find that I was at least as much to be pitied myself.

MICHEL DE MONTAIGNE: *ESSAYS* (TRANSLATED BY J M COHEN)

The years after Igor's birth at the end of 1980 had been happy ones. The only cause we had for regret was my seeming inability to get pregnant again and see Edna's reading come true: that I would have another boy and a little girl. We had to wait until the summer of 1985, when we had more or less given up hope of having another child.

My daughter Jana was born on 18th March 1986, half an hour after midnight. The doctor and midwives all around me looked very surprised when I kept repeating 'It's a girl!' with such delirious joy. The second son I had been expecting was never to be born. Goran and I were only ever to have two children: Ig and Jana. Later I was to reflect that Edna had said she saw pictures from my life. She may well have seen Ig with his best friend Fidan – they were as inseparable as brothers.

Meanwhile Goran had become a famous and prolific playwright throughout Yugoslavia, with many accolades to his name, all the highest honours the theatre and the state could give him. He left the English Department to set up a Playwriting Department in the Faculty of Dramatic Arts the year Jana was born. He hadn't done much work on the PhD he had started researching when we were in Manchester, preferring to write plays rather than do academic research. He was awarded Outstanding Artist Fulbright Scholar status with a six-month scholarship to spend at Brown University, Providence, Rhode Island in the United States. At the beginning of 1990 we flew to New York from Belgrade and on to Providence in a small propeller plane.

Our six months in Providence were enjoyable and rewarding. We made several good friends and both our children became highly proficient speakers of English as well as Macedonian. But when we returned, a realisation was slowly dawning. Although many had been gloomy about the prospects for maintaining the famous 'brotherhood and unity' of Yugoslavia after Tito's death, I had always been an optimist and never seriously considered that such a successful state, which had found a happy medium between West and East in Europe, would fail. Being an internationalist, I hadn't reckoned with the resurgent nationalism in the Balkan states.

My husband's generation were mainly true Yugoslavs – they didn't know or care if, for example, a Bosnian friend had a Serbian, Croatian or Bosniak background. It was irrelevant. But there were those of the older generation for whom the atrocities of the Second World War were still alive. The Croat Ustaše had had their own state under the Axis powers and many Serbs living in Croatia had been murdered. There were also Serbs and Croats who thought Bosnia should cease to exist and be split between them. I began to be aware of a black cloud slowly approaching to eclipse our simple happy lives in Yugoslavia. Nationalist leaders had taken over in Serbia and Croatia, with the parliament of the Croatian Republic removing the term 'socialist' from their title and adopting a new constitution. This prompted the Serbian enclave of Knin in Croatia to secede and set up their own autonomous region.

In the late spring of 1991, a few months after these events, I attended a two-week advanced-level course on generative grammar at the Inter-University Centre in Dubrovnik on the Croatian coast. There were linguists from all over the world. It was stimulating to have two weeks to be myself without family duties and discuss topics I found fascinating with like-minded people. We spent many an interesting hour in local cafés and the last evening went to a fish restaurant by the sea for a slap-up meal. We were sitting outside. At one point, loud bangs echoed from the mountains behind us. I said what we were all thinking, trying to sound light-hearted:

'Don't worry. It's just the war starting.'

The worrying noises stopped and we tried to distract ourselves by talking about anything but politics. Somehow the conversation turned to astrology and palmistry. There was an Indian man there, who said he could indeed read our palms. With nothing better to do, we took turns holding out our hands for him to look at in a spirit of joking disbelief. He told my colleagues various things about their lives, nothing unusual, just about their love lives, children and interests. Then it came to me. I remember only one thing he said about my palm.

'Oh,' he declared, 'you nearly died around the age of thirty.'

I laughed.

'I think I might remember that!' I said.

He gave me a strange look and continued with someone else.

We all returned home the next day. It turned out the war had indeed started, or at least the initial skirmishes. I found it all extremely unsettling and disturbing. I still couldn't believe that there would really be a civil war, that the nations of Yugoslavia would actually start fighting each other. Mum had told me at the age of ten that there would never be another war. She said the Second World War had been so terrible, it had been the war to end all wars (I didn't know at the time that was what they'd said about World War I). The idea of a war between all the friendly people I'd met all over Yugoslavia was just as unimaginable as England and Scotland going to war with each other.

Not long after I got back from Dubrovnik, there was a family celebration at Uncle Risto's. A friend and neighbour was there. She had been the anaesthetist during my Caesarean, but our paths rarely crossed. On this occasion we were thrown together in the hall as we were both leaving.

'Ah, Patricia,' she said, pinching my cheek, 'it's so good to see you looking so alive and well. We thought we'd lost you, you know.'

I was dumbfounded. She saw my shocked expression and went on.

'We didn't tell you at the time, but something happened

during the Caesarean. You died for a few moments. Luckily, we managed to bring you back.'

I thought soberly of the Indian linguist who'd read my palm and apologised to him mentally. I had been thirty-one when I had the Caesarean – around the age of thirty as he had said. But how could he have seen that in my palm? How could there possibly be information like that in the lines on your hand? It was ridiculous and yet he had seen it. It wasn't something he said to anyone else, either. And the recollection of looking down at myself on the operating table from up by the electric heater during my Caesarean came back in vivid clarity.

☙

So, the lines on your palm really do map out your life. No one is quite sure of the origins of palmistry, but it probably originated in my fellow linguist's nation of India, thought to have its roots in Hindu astrology and to have spread to Roma fortune tellers. That made me remember another palm-reading in my life.

One day I had been alone at home as a teenager when a Roma woman knocked on the door selling tea-towels. I told her Mum was out and that I had no money to give her. She accepted the truth of this good-naturedly and offered to read my palm. After what seemed like a cursory glance, she told me that I would be a teacher and that I would live in a foreign land. Both things were to turn out to be true.

These days palmistry is commonly regarded as harmless fun by most people, but no less a philosopher than Aristotle put faith in it. He apparently found a treatise on palmistry on an altar of Hermes. He later gave it to his pupil Alexander the Great, who is said to have taken it very seriously and set great store by it when analysing his officers' characters from the lines on their hands.

Palmistry seems to have been in vogue at the end of the 19th century and beginning of the 20th century. Cheiro, an Irishman whose real name was William Warner, studied it in India and set up a practice in London. His famous clients included Oscar Wilde, William Gladstone, Joseph Chamberlain and an initially sceptical Mark Twain, who declared that Cheiro had in fact revealed his character to him with an accuracy which was humiliating.

My experience was only with what my life line shows and what my future was to be, not with my character. The 100% accuracy on those two occasions means I have to accept that there is obviously something in palmistry and presumably in other ancient traditions which have survived the test of time.

As for my out-of-body experience (OBE), seeing myself on the operating table, it is a well-known part of a near-death experience (NDE). The film *Flatliners* plays on popular knowledge of such experiences. It concerns five medical students who explore the realm of near-death experiences as each has his or her heart stopped for a short time and is then revived. It turns into a horror film which departs from the kind of experiences reported in reality.

In his book *To Die For*, Beichler informs us that near-death experiences are the same all over the world and do not vary according to the religion, age, level of education or any other factor of those who have them. Apart from the OBE, they can include going through a dark tunnel towards the light, feelings of great peace and being given the choice of whether to return to one's body or not. From his research, Beichler discovered that those who go further than just floating above their bodies and actually see the light experience a transformation in their personalities to become 'much more psychic, compassionate and ecologically aware'.

Interestingly, I experienced another feature of a NDE when I was in North Wales in 1973. I was driving down a mountain in the dark and rain when suddenly my headlights picked out a human figure on the road. I swerved to the side of the road to avoid them and lost control of the car. I saw my whole life flash before me in the moment it took for the car to spin and end up facing the other way. Beichler states that this past-life review doesn't have to be part of a NDE – I didn't die at any point during this event.

Various explanations of OBEs and NDEs have been presented by scientists. They could be mechanisms produced by the mind to protect it from facing death, or a chemical reaction in the brain caused by the brain shutting down. The hallucinogenic drug ketamine can also apparently induce out-of-body experiences and other near-death experiences. Beichler refers to a Dr Susan Blackmore, who had herself had a near-death experience. She devoted several years to investigating what had happened and concluded it was the effects of the dying brain and of reanimating it. Beichler doesn't accept this and points out that people who die suddenly and unexpectedly for a short time have the same experiences as those who don't actually die at all.

If I relate my own out-of-body experience to my other paranormal experiences, it seems to confirm that we must have at least two 'bodies', or a body and a soul, if you will. Sometimes the second body doesn't have the physical form it does in 'ghosts of the living'.

8.

What a coincidence!: 1993

Synchronicity and morphic resonance

We live in our description of reality.

GREGORY BATESON

On 25th June 1991, Slovenia and Croatia had declared independence from Yugoslavia and the Slovenes took over the border posts with Italy, Austria and Hungary. The Yugoslav National Army tried to take back the borders and shots were exchanged. The Slovenian War lasted only ten days before an agreement was made to allow the Slovenes to go their own way.

Peace was short-lived, however; the Yugoslav National Army and Serb paramilitaries turned their attention to Croatia. In August, the siege of Vukovar began, a city on the Danube, the border with Serbia running down the middle of the river. Over the following three months we watched the horrific bombardment of the city on the television news reports. Fewer than 2,000 people defended it against 36,000 soldiers and paramilitaries. The city was reduced to mainly rubble. There were rumours of sickening atrocities when the army and paramilitaries finally entered it, grenades thrown into basements where women and children were sheltering, men bussed out and murdered in their hundreds in the countryside.

Not long after this horror, Dubrovnik was besieged and bombarded. This really caught the attention of the international media; the damage to Dubrovnik was minimal in comparison to the devastation of Vukovar, but many Western Europeans had been to the attractive Adriatic city on holiday and it was a UNESCO World Heritage site. It was painful to think of it bombarded and under siege.

We tried to get on with our lives as if nothing was really happening that could affect us. I went to a language conference in Sofia, Bulgaria, and made a presentation about teaching English conditionals. Afterwards I was approached by a teacher from Pilgrims English Language School in Canterbury; the School was well-known and respected in the profession and the teacher had written some famous books on TEFL. I took the opportunity of being interviewed by him for a job teaching on the summer school in Canterbury that year and was contacted by Pilgrims soon afterwards to say they needed me for two months to teach the English for Teachers course.

6th April 1992 was the day I think I finally realised there was not going to be a future for us in Yugoslavia. It was the day Serbian snipers shot into the crowd of tens of thousands of peace protestors in Sarajevo. The two young women who were killed were the first victims of the siege of that city, which was to last three times longer than Stalingrad and a year longer than Leningrad in the Second World War. As the spring went by with pictures of terrified citizens dodging bullets on their city streets, my despair grew.

On 4th July we flew to London and went to stay with Dad for a week. He had had lumps in his left arm which had been removed, and I was worried about what was actually wrong with him. I was relieved to find he seemed to be well, although I wasn't satisfied with his dismissal of the lumps in his arm as harmless. He drove us down to Canterbury so I could take up my summer teaching job.

Our first view of Canterbury from the top of the hill as we came from the A2 was stupendous, the cathedral dominating the scene, the sun sparkling on the windows, little medieval houses surrounding it. I remembered my first sight of it on a visit with Noelle from Folkestone nearly twenty years before and felt as if I was coming home. It took us a very long time to find the house at 1, King Street where we were staying – the one-way system was confusing for strangers to say the least – but we eventually located it and settled in.

It was in that old house with its slanting floors and creaking stairs that I finally plucked up courage six weeks later to tell Goran I couldn't go back to Skopje.

I don't think I myself understood the enormity of what I was saying. Goran was a famous writer in Yugoslavia, more or less a household name in Macedonia. An Englishwoman I met on the course in Dubrovnik told me he had been described to her in Croatia as 'The Yugoslav Shakespeare'. He was also a man who was very tied to his roots, his language and his culture. I, on the other hand, was happy wherever I was, provided I was with the people I loved.

I had taken Yugoslav citizenship in addition to my British one – this meant having two passports with which I could get into most countries in the world without a visa. In Skopje Goran's close and extended family had happily accepted me and treated me as their own. I had a job I enjoyed and had built up a reputation as a linguist whose articles and papers were praised and valued. The friends I had made were the closest I have ever had.

So, the declaration I made to Goran that evening in Canterbury was truly momentous and life-changing. He was profoundly shaken by it and, of course, tried to dissuade me. But I stood my ground. Had we not had children, perhaps I would have taken my chances going back to that war-torn country. By then, Macedonia had also declared its independence from Yugoslavia but very few people thought Slobodan Milošević, the President of the rump Yugoslavia, which now consisted just of Serbia and Montenegro, would allow any republic to secede without consequences. It was just a matter of time before he got round to dealing with Macedonia.

What future was there for my children in that country? I was putting them in harm's way by taking them back. We could make a new life in my own homeland.

Finally, Goran said we would stay in England if I could find a job. By chance, the School of English Studies in Folkestone of happy memory was advertising for a teacher and an English school for business people in Canterbury also needed a full-time trainer. I went for interviews at both. The Folkestone school could only offer a temporary contract for one term whereas the Director of Canterbury Language Training offered me a permanent contract. I took the job, even though I didn't much fancy teaching Business English. Goran's condition for staying in the country was fulfilled.

Had I known then that it would take six long years before Goran stopped dividing his life between Skopje, Stockholm and Canterbury, I might have hesitated, but I thought it would just be a temporary arrangement until he had finished with the group of students he was in the middle of guiding through their four years of study at the time.

As well as teaching blocks of lectures in Skopje, Goran started work on a project in Stockholm. His friend, the distinguished theatre historian Dragan Klaić, had left Belgrade and made a new life in Amsterdam as Director of the Dutch Theatre Institute. Klaia, as everyone called him, had fingers in every cultural pie in Europe. He linked Goran up with Chris Torch, an Italian-American theatre director and producer living and working in Stockholm. Chris was involved with the events for Antwerp as Cultural City of Europe in 1993. He commissioned Goran to write a play about Sarajevo to be directed by a Bosnian exile, Haris Pašović. They were to work together in Stockholm that autumn, rehearsing the play for Antwerp the following year.

A Scandinavian winter with its few hours of light and constant greyness was not the best of environments for two Yugoslav exiles in the midst of their grief and trauma to spend much time with no close friends or family around. Goran wrote his elegiac *Sarajevo – Tales from a City*, but Haris couldn't reconcile himself to having left his home city to its fate. At the end of the year, he gave up on the project and actually smuggled himself back into the besieged city, which most of its inhabitants dreamed of leaving. He was to become a key figure in creating and participating in numerous productions and events to raise awareness of the outrage of what was happening in Sarajevo.

Chris agreed to a new director for Goran's play: Slobodan Unkovski - Unko, who had directed most of his plays in Macedonia. They stuck out the Swedish winter together and the resulting production toured various places in Europe after the run in Antwerp. In the UK it had several performances at the Riverside Studios in Hammersmith and in Cambridge.

We had by then got into a routine of Goran coming to

stay with us for a couple of weeks every two months or so. Those were terrible years for our little family. The nightly news brought no respite from the daily horror of the atrocities in Bosnia. I knew it wasn't good for the children to see me weeping in front of the TV news, but I felt it my duty to the land I had loved and called my own to go on following its fate and the suffering of those I had seen as compatriots. We were trying to make a new life in England, but it was impossible to escape what was happening where our old life had been.

I suppose it was lucky that my new job was very demanding. At Canterbury Language Training, six hours a day were devoted to teaching English to business people from all over the world. No two clients were ever the same, even if they worked for the same company in the same department. I had to learn a great deal about all sectors of all kinds of industry, financial as well as manufacturing. It got to the point where the bankers thought I was an economist because of the English terms I taught them and the issues we discussed cribbed from The Financial Times or some such publication, the engineers thought I was really into technology for the same reason, while the journalists knew I was one of them as I was so completely au fait with current affairs.

But it was heartbreaking that my job allowed me no holidays in the summer and my children had to attend summer camps. I was getting near to a nervous breakdown.

But Fate stepped in to save me. By some strange chance, my client had to return home the very morning of Jana's sports day at her primary school and I could take the afternoon off. I couldn't wait to get there and be a proper mum, watching my child running and jumping alongside the other mums and dads.

It was a sunny afternoon and the playground was packed. Eventually a woman saw me looking for a seat and moved up on her bench so I could sit beside her. We soon got talking. Her name was Caroline and we became friends, having coffee together quite a few times after that day.

It turned out Caroline was a counsellor, and she gave me generously of her time and support over those coffees without expecting me to pay for her professional services, which I could never have afforded at that time. It was not long after we'd taken on a mortgage and Goran was still commuting from Skopje, both of us with low salaries for the cost of living in our new home. Caroline kept me sane during the bad times and we had got to know each other simply by the coincidence of sitting next to each other at a school sports day.

It was a Spanish businessman at Canterbury Language Training who made me think more about the coincidences in life, which really are too frequent and fantastic to be just coincidences. He had been to London for the weekend and recounted what happened when he got off a Tube train at Oxford Circus. The platform was crowded. As he shuffled his way to the exit, he kicked something on the ground. He looked down to see what it was and saw a woman's purse. Having picked it up, he opened it to find some form of identification which would help in returning it to its owner. Imagine his amazement when it turned out to belong to his best friend's sister. He was able to call her and tell her he had her purse!

I could write a whole book about the strange coincidences I've experienced or heard about in my life, but let me just recount the most memorable to make my point.

Since I retired from teaching, I have become more involved

in my community and campaigning on local issues. One such campaign was against the closure of the Whitstable Royal Mail Sorting Office. The main instigator was a woman called Julie Wassmer, and we became friends.

Julie is first and foremost a writer and it was as an author that she had the truly astounding experience which she recounts in her book, *More Than Just Coincidence*. She tells how she went to the offices of a London agent one day to interest her in a book she was writing. They had a good meeting and the agent said she would represent Julie's book to publishers. The following day, she called Julie unexpectedly. She said she had something to tell her of a personal nature and she didn't quite know how to broach it. Julie asked her to go on. The agent told her she had an assistant working with her that week who had been seconded from another office to help while her own assistant was away. The temporary assistant had been typing out the details of the agreement with Julie and recognised her name as that of her birth mother. Did this make any sense to Julie? Could the young woman contact her?

Julie was overcome with emotion. When she was seventeen, she had given birth to a daughter, knowing her baby would be adopted as she couldn't look after the child herself. In one memorable and moving detail, she recalls how she had bought a little outfit for the baby to send with her to her adopted parents but had watched as a nurse dropped the outfit in a bin. The Sixties were still a cruel time for unmarried mothers.

At the time the agent called her, Julie was happily married but had never had another child. She often thought of her little girl and wondered what had become of her. Had she been to see the London agent any other week, her daughter would never have seen her name, never have got in touch. It was truly a remarkable coincidence.

My friend Peggy's sister Judy told me about another staggering incident, which again beggars belief. A friend of hers needed to contact her son one day when he was in London, before mobile phones. He had given her the phone number of where he was staying so she called the number and asked for him. He came to the phone very puzzled.

'How did you find me here?' he asked.

'Well, you gave me this number,' she replied.

'I gave you the number of where I'm staying,' he replied, 'but I'm not there. I'm in a meeting at a company in town.'

Amazingly, his mother had dialled the number of that company instead of the one she had planned to dial.

A similar incident was recounted on a Saturday morning programme on Radio Four recently. A man went into a phone box to call someone but the phone rang before he could dial the number. He picked it up since he couldn't use the phone without answering the call; it turned out to be a friend of his, who thought he was calling his home number.

Then there's my friend, Glenn, an anthropologist who did his fieldwork in a Palestinian village where he got to know people well. Last year he and Elizabeth were visiting Orvieto, not a town much on the tourist trail in Italy. There were very few people around. On one narrow street a young woman came up to them and asked them for directions. They got talking and established she was Palestinian. She came from the same village where Glenn had lived and he knew her family.

ᴄᴑ

When you begin to notice the coincidences in your everyday life you realise just how common they are – far too common to be called coincidences. In his article 'The Uncanny', Freud states that 'all obsessional neurotics I have observed are able to relate analogous experiences like running into the person you were just thinking of, getting a letter from that person the next day – presentiments which 'usually' come true.'

I don't think I can, by any stretch of the imagination, classify everyone of my acquaintance who has told me about the coincidences they have experienced in their lives as 'obsessional neurotics'. And Freud's explanation seems sweeping: '...the uncanny is nothing else than a hidden familiar thing that has undergone repression and then emerged from it, and (that) everything that is uncanny fulfils this condition'. However, the great psychoanalyst apparently changed his mind. In his unpublished 1921 article 'Psychoanalysis and Telepathy', he states: 'it no longer seems possible to brush aside the study of so-called occult facts,' by which he meant the real existence of psychic forces.

In 1902 Carl Jung had presented his doctoral thesis entitled 'On the Psychology and Pathology of So-Called Occult Phenomena'; it was a psychological study of a medium. Later he was to recount the stunning coincidence of a patient recounting her dream about someone giving her a golden scarab as a present. At that very moment, Jung heard something tapping at the window. He opened the window to let in a common rose chafer, a beetle closely resembling a golden scarab. He termed this amazing coincidence 'synchronicity', defined as 'the acausal connection of two or more psychic and physical phenomena'.

A convincing explanation of this synchronicity in the kind of coincidences we have been discussing is the notion of morphic resonance. I happened to see a TV programme about biologist Rupert Sheldrake many years ago; he had developed the theory around it. It posits a kind of resonance between similar people, brought together by some kind of attraction, or vibration. A feasible explanation of the coincidences we experience would be this kind of consciousness among individuals who are linked in some way, whether it be a family relationship or a similarity of experience or character. People are literally 'drawn to each other'.

To illustrate this very quickly, a couple of years ago I attended a reading by the author Jane Gardam in the yurt set up in the Franciscan Gardens by the Wise Words festival organisers. I was one of the first to arrive and took my place on a bench near the centre. Looking around, I decided after a few minutes to move to a chair with a cushion on it near the entrance as I have some problems with my back and felt it needed some support. The yurt filled up and soon there were few places left, two of them on chairs next to me. A rather elegant couple came in – the woman looked to be in her late forties. She asked if the seats next to me were free and I told her they were. She sat down and we got talking. It turned out she was doing the creative writing course at Canterbury Christ Church University, and Jane Gardam's work had been recommended to her. I expressed my own love of Jane's work. Soon it was clear that the woman was in a state of anxiety. She told me her cameraman son, who was working for an American TV company, was shortly going out to Syria and she was worried about his safety in that war-torn country.

Not long after I had moved my seat, I saw Patrick Cockburn,

the distinguished Independent journalist, come in and take the very seat in the centre I had left unoccupied. We smiled at each other and said Hello in recognition, as I had attended his talk the day before in the same place and had asked a question. His theme was *Isis & how politicians duck the blame for terrorism.* From the talk, I knew Patrick had spent a great deal of time in Syria during the course of the war there. Without more ado, I went over to him and told him about my neighbour's concerns, asking him if he could speak to her and reassure her about her son's safety. He agreed and, during the interval for tea, he had a long talk with her, telling her about the elaborate safety and security measures taken for journalists and their crews. As a result, she looked much relieved and thanked me profusely for having put her in touch with Patrick.

It was difficult not to think that this woman had been 'drawn' to me, somehow aware that I could help her and that I had, in fact, changed my place in the yurt to be of use to her. I could almost feel the vibrations of morphic resonance at work, which I'd hardly been aware of that time I'd sat down next to Caroline at Jana's school sports day and been rescued from the very dark place I had been entering.

9

The tap with a mind of its own: 1994
Poltergeists and spirits

Consider this, though: We can't see radio waves, but we know they exist. Spirits just vibrate at a frequency well above the visible range — that tiny sliver of the electromagnetic spectrum of energy that defines our reality.

DR ELISA MEDHUS, MINDBODYGREEN.COM

A contributing factor to the breakdown I had narrowly averted in our first years in Canterbury was my concern about Dad. He had left his quiet, comfortable life near his sister in Pershore and joined us in the rented house by the river we took in Canterbury. He slept on a camp bed in the study, picked Jana up from school every day and made tea for her and Ig. He was eighty years old but he seemed to think nothing of uprooting himself and coming to our aid.

What self-sacrifice! I didn't fully appreciate what he was doing at the time; I was so absorbed in the heart-breaking situation we were in. When I was home, when we had guests, Dad would spend most of the time reading a book in a corner of the living room, not intruding on our lives, yet there when needed. He became a popular regular at The Unicorn pub up the road and a well-loved grandpa at home. He also had appointments set up for him with a consultant at Kent &

Canterbury Hospital. According to him, there was nothing much wrong with him. But his health was becoming even more of a worry as he seemed to be losing the use of his left arm. One day he told me the doctor had advised him to stop driving as he could hardly change gear. He turned the ownership of his red Renault 19 over to me with philosophical forbearance.

Growing ever more suspicious about his true state of health, I arranged to go and see his specialist at the hospital without his knowledge. To my shock and indignation, the specialist stated he had wondered how long it would take before someone from the family would come and see him. He then said straight out that Dad had a brain tumour and he gave him three months to live. He declared that Dad didn't know, and that he wouldn't want to know. I managed to remonstrate with him a little, but the specialist said patronisingly that he knew best. I was too upset to ask any more questions and just left the room as quickly as I could, not managing to keep back the tears until I was outside. A kindly nurse steered me into a space away from the waiting patients – no doubt it was something she regularly did after most appointments with that consultant. A cup of tea appeared soon after I had sat down and a soothing hand on my arm.

The next three months were fraught and stressful. Many times I thought of telling Dad the consultant's diagnosis, but such was my awe of the medical profession and my own lack of self-confidence that I didn't do it. This didn't stop me from reflecting every night that I would want to know if I had a brain tumour so I could put my affairs in order and perhaps do something I'd wanted to do all my life but had never done.

Something on my bucket list. Why do they call it that? Is it something to do with kicking the bucket?

To my tremendous relief, Dad gradually came to realise that he couldn't look after himself anymore and decided to move into a care home. We looked at various places. A room in the beautiful Old Rectory in Ickham, a village six miles east of Canterbury, finally came up and I drove Dad over there with his now modest possessions to move in. He had a garden room, which was wonderful. He'd been a keen gardener all his life, so it was a happy chance that he had that garden room at The Old Rectory.

Dad had been in his new home less than a month, however, when the manager rang to tell me he had been taken to hospital. He had suddenly become incontinent and was not well. We rushed to see him in the Kent & Canterbury up the hill. He was still completely lucid and thought he had some bug, which would mean he was out again soon and back in his lovely room.

Ten days later, he was no better, but remembered Jana's eighth birthday was coming up on 18th March. Dad gave me some money, asking me to buy her a big box of crayons from him. She loved drawing. On the following Sunday, two days after Jana's birthday, my brother Richard came down to visit. We spent the whole afternoon with Dad. He was still putting a brave face on things and talking about how he was going to live at least another six years, like his own father, or even another sixteen, like my great aunt May. It was almost exactly three months since I had seen the consultant.

In the mid-afternoon Dad started complaining of a bad pain in his leg. We called the nurse over and she went off to discuss pain relief with the on-duty doctor. It was two hours later when the injection finally arrived and the doctor asked Richard and me to go to her office with her to talk. But we'd only just sat down when the nurse came rushing in and said 'He's going!' and we ran back to Dad's bedside.

He had gone. I kissed him and held his hand, bursting into tears. Richard got me up and steered me out and to the car. We drove back in silence to a house where Goran was comforting two weeping children. The hospital had phoned ahead with the news.

Ten days later, the schools broke up for Easter and Igor and Jana were at home alone, while I was at work and Goran was out. Jana started watching a TV programme about ghosts while Igor was still in bed upstairs. She became more and more scared and was petrified with horror when one of the living-room curtains suddenly billowed out and formed the shape of a man over the armchair. Jana screamed and ran upstairs to get Igor. He came downstairs and bravely approached the curtain, which fell back into place when he touched it. The window wasn't open and there was no draught.

The next evening, we were all having dinner in the dining room when we heard the tap in the kitchen next door turn full on. I went and turned it off, checking that it was not dripping, or in any way faulty. The following evening, the same thing happened, but this time it was later in the evening and I was the only one in the dining room to hear the water gushing from the tap. I went into the kitchen and closed the door behind me. When I had turned off the tap, I stood in the middle of the room and spoke quietly but evenly.

'Dad,' I said, 'it's all right. Just go towards the light.'

I suppose it was a line from a film or a ghost story I'd read and I felt very silly saying those words, but the strange happenings in the house stopped and there were no more ghostly occurrences.

The month before Dad died, one of the worst atrocities of the Siege of Sarajevo took place. The mortar which hit a market stall on 5th February 1994 killed 68 and injured 144. But even the marketplace atrocity in 1994 didn't prepare me for the capitulation of the Dutch troops in the UN 'safe haven' of Srebrenica in July the following year and the subsequent massacre of more than 7,000 Muslim men and boys there by the Bosnian Serb army under Ratko Mladić. I went down with a virus which I couldn't throw off and spent weeks off work. My colleague John rightly dubbed it The Srebrenica 'Flu. I coughed for months afterwards and experienced the worst period of depression I've ever known in my generally happy life.

The Nineties were a time both Goran and I rarely mention. They were characterised by a mechanical, robotic getting through each day without thinking too much, trying not to look to the future or reflect on the past, just get the kids off to school in the morning, go to work, earn enough money by teaching, writing reports and marking video presentations, while Goran went on teaching in Skopje and coming to Canterbury every six weeks for a fortnight. My heart still aches when I think of that time and my throat tightens. We wanted and needed Goran with us all the time, but he couldn't give up his job and his country, or choose between his family and his roots.

So it was that I dismissed the ghostly experiences in our house in 1994 with everything else that was going on and put them to the back of my mind. But they must have worked away somewhere in my subconscious to make me want to explore further in this area, forbidden fruit for anyone of my education and background.

Now that I'm writing this book, I went to the Spiritualist Church in Canterbury for an evening with a clairvoyant. I was hoping to get some inkling of how a medium/clairvoyant works and whether she really is in touch with spirits.

There were three Church staff at the meeting: a taciturn, cross-looking middle-aged woman with thin brown plaits, who I hardly heard speak all evening, and two middle-aged men with dyed black hair, who did contribute a little to the proceedings. The audience consisted of me and four youngish women, all members of one family. Disappointment was expressed at the unusually low turnout.

The clairvoyant turned up just before 7.30pm, when the event was due to start. She and the man with her apologised and blamed the traffic. The clairvoyant, Ann Farmer, looked middle-aged, though when I spoke to her at the end, she said she was seventy. She wasn't slim or plump – just rather on the heavy side. She had blonde shoulder-length hair, pleasant features and blue eyes. Ann was wearing a long floaty navy shirt of some artificial material with big white and pink flowers on it over navy blue trousers.

After a short prayer, Ann set to work and started with me. This was rather unexpected – I had been hoping to remain more of an observer of proceedings. She was rather nervous and halting but said she had a gentleman talking to her – my father? – telling her he had problems in the chest area, soon specified as the lungs, and that he had been hospitalised not long before his death.

This was quite surprising, as Dad had in fact known he

had lung cancer, but not that he had a brain tumour, which is what had actually killed him. Ann correctly said Dad had smoked a pipe when I was growing up and talked about the plaque my brother and I had had made with Dad's name and dates to add to the family vault in Offley churchyard. She then mentioned daffodils, which took me back to the ones he had planted all along the border in the garden, visible from our back window, and how they had been in full bloom when he died. There had also been a host of them waving in the breeze as we emerged from the crematorium where his funeral service had taken place.

'He says you like flowers, too – especially red roses,' Ann went on. Dad would have remembered how I had not rested till I found a fragrant red standard rose for that same border where the daffodils had come up in such numbers. The colour and the perfume had been the two most important points for the rose.

'Your mother has passed over, too, hasn't she? She wasn't well but her death wasn't expected. She loved yellow roses,' continued Ann. This was all getting a bit much. Although Mum had had angina for some years, her fatal heart attack in hospital at the age of sixty-six when I had been at home for the summer was indeed a shock; and, yes, she had loved yellow roses.

'They're together now,' said Ann, 'and they're fine. They're often with you. Your Mum holds you in her arms when you're going through a bad time.'

This brought on the tears. I had a vivid memory of an evening when Ig was only two months old soon after we had found out my father-in-law Mirko had lung cancer. Goran and his brother Vlatko had gone to Belgrade with their father for him to have a lung removed at the prestigious Army Hospital there.

I felt very alone and desperate during those weeks. I had never regained my usual cheery disposition after the birth; perhaps I was suffering from some kind of post-natal depression.

One evening it had reached its nadir and my thoughts were black. I was trying to breastfeed Ig as instructed, even though I had very little milk to give him. I was sitting on one side of the bed while I was doing this.

Suddenly, I felt a tremendous feeling of warmth and joy sweep over me. I knew Mum and Mirko were sitting at the bottom of the bed. I didn't turn to look at them – I just knew they were there, smiling at me. From that day on, I was stronger, physically and mentally, and much calmer and more confident that I could be a good mother.

'You're fighting with yourself – does that make sense?' asked Ann. I could only nod. 'But now you're finally putting two and two together and making four.' She paused.

Then she said emphatically: 'Awareness – that's the word. Do you meditate? Are you in a circle? You're a healer. You heal people simply with your calmness, the way you listen to them. You have spirit guides around you.'

There was more about how my parents saw me. This woman didn't say a word out of place.

Ann moved on to the family at the back. I quickly wrote down the things she had said about me and then listened to what she was saying. The young women's grandmother was getting in touch. There was a cat with her. I perked my ears up at that – so my ginger cat Sandy could well have gone on to an afterlife.

After the event I went up to speak to Ann. She clearly was communicating with the spirits of the dead and she had astounded me with what she had said about me. She couldn't have been reading my thoughts as I wasn't thinking about my Dad or expecting him to get in touch, even less so my Mum, who had died forty years earlier. With her phrase 'fighting with myself' Ann had put her finger on what I had been doing for nearly fifty years of my life, developing a philosophy of life completely at odds with my paranormal experiences. I was finally coming to an awareness, as she said.

In answer to my questions, I discovered that Ann had only been a platform medium for three years. She had always had an interest in the supernatural but had only come to spiritualism in her forties, when her children needed her less. She had then trained to be a medium – she hadn't always heard the voices of spirits. They had slowly come to her, though she wished they would speak a bit more loudly as if on the telephone. They transmitted feelings and emotions to her as well – she would feel pain in her chest from a heart attack, breathing trouble from lung cancer. She must also be seeing them in some sense, as she mentioned the fact that my father had shown her a breathing apparatus to make it clear he had trouble breathing.

❧

A close friend of mine has told me about an experience of hers with a clairvoyant, which really does indicate that the woman was also genuinely communicating with the dead.

My friend was a teacher in a secondary school and, at the time of this incident, had planned to have a hysterectomy in the summer term, which would inevitably have led to several weeks of rest and recuperation.

Some weeks before the date of the operation, a colleague came into the staff room with some extraordinary events from the weekend to relate. The colleague had been to a Psychic Fair and had paid £10 for a reading, only to have the clairvoyant insist that she pass on a message to my friend. She went on to say that older women in my friend's family were determined to persuade her to arrange for a cleaner when she came out of hospital – otherwise they feared, in their Lancashire phrase, that she would 'put herself back' ie do too much too soon. My friend could almost hear the women in her family speaking in this way, loving but pragmatic and unsentimental.

Thus instructed, she did indeed find someone to help in the short term. In the longer term this person came to act as a loved friend and housekeeper to her elderly parents, enabling my friend to go on working and providing essential support and care for the whole family.

This incident seems to provide convincing proof that the dead are still among us in some invisible form and see what we are doing. Nevertheless, this evidence is difficult to accept, not just from the rational point of view but from an emotional standpoint: how disconcerting, to say the least, to know we are constantly under surveillance by some sort of spirits, rather like the children in Pullman's Cittàgazze, unaware of the dreadful Spectres all around them!

My friend's dead relations were desperate to communicate with her and kept an eye out for the right opportunity. They clearly knew where she worked and who her colleagues were and used the medium of the clairvoyant to contact her through her colleague. On hearing the message from her colleague, my friend said it was typical of her aunts' protectiveness and what they would have said to her if they had been alive.

This communication from the dead is also typical of the ones you hear about. It seems to be rare that someone communicates anything of vital importance from beyond the grave (the film *Ghost* was, after all, fiction). Normally, they just continue with the conversation interrupted by their death.

My friend's experience is all the more convincing as it was so indirect. It certainly indicates that the psychic was genuinely communicating something she heard rather than making something up which she thought her client wanted to hear. This case, called a drop-in in the literature, is the most convincing since it proves beyond doubt that the medium is not mind-reading the client.

I think it's time to face head-on the class element involved in mediumship and interest in the spirit world. I felt this almost palpably when I attended the Spiritualist Church in Canterbury. Neither practitioners nor congregation were middle-class people and this provides another unspoken barrier to such people becoming involved, at least in our still oh-so-class-bound society in England.

I dare to mention this point as I find backing from Roger Clarke in his *A Natural History of Ghosts*: 'The middle classes have always deplored the idea of ghosts. Professional sceptics are usually drawn from this strata (*sic*) of society. Your middle-class sceptic would say that toffs like ghosts because it is a symptom of their decadence, the plebeians because they are ill-educated.'[15]

Clarke notes that studies since the 1940s have shown that it has become more socially acceptable to say one believes in

15.   p.173

ghosts, but my discomfort about writing this book can definitely be attributed not just to my level of education and that of my friends, but also to my (reluctant) sense of class belonging.

One positive side to all this, though, is that all the incidents I've related here were of the dead giving help and consolation to us living. In my case, when I had such a strong sense of my mother and father-in-law sitting on the end of the bed radiating their love and support to me when I most needed it, my father-in-law was in fact not yet dead but in an operating theatre hundreds of miles away in Belgrade. Was this another case of bilocation, as I experienced in Folkestone, where the bioplasma body separates from the physical body when strong emotion requires?

In the case of my father, his apparent inability to accept that he was dead, which made his spirit draw our attention by turning on the tap in the kitchen, ties in with much of what one reads about people who die unexpectedly. He hadn't known about his brain tumour and, on the day he died, was talking about how many more years he was going to live.

In the Tibetan culture, the Bardo Thodol, the Tibetan Book of the Dead, is actually read out over the body of a dead person to guide him or her through the afterworld, so it is assumed that the dead person can still hear living people speaking. The soul is at first disoriented and confused from the loss of its body and needs guidance. Upon death, it enters the 'Clear Light of Ultimate Reality' and, if it can recognise this reality, it will achieve liberation from rebirth, called *moksha* and *nirvana*. There are six different lokas, or worlds of reality, each with its own light, which the soul can journey through. Going towards the light is the classic experience of many near-death experiences, and most religions see their 'Heaven' as a place of bright light.

To return to the living actually communicating with the dead, the general public is often sceptical about mediums doing this, believing they all rely on 'cold reading' techniques. This involves the so-called medium throwing out names, initials or images and waiting for a reaction from sitters. When this comes, they produce more details about the deceased person until they again receive a reaction. The details they provide are general and could apply to many people, which is why they tend to seem successful to the gullible. These 'mediums' are involved in a form of trickery and even sometimes call themselves 'psychic magicians'.

However, the fact that some mediums are genuine has gained credibility through the research of Dr Gary Schwartz in Tucson, Arizona, and the book he subsequently published called *The Afterlife Experiments*.

Dr Schwartz has had a distinguished career and a wealth of papers published in reputable journals. When it came to finding mediums to take part in his experiments, most so-called mediums refused as soon as they were told they would not be able to see the sitter in some of the experiments. Schwartz makes a clear distinction between mediums who do 'cold reading' and those who are apparently genuinely receiving communications from the dead. He found four professional mediums and one amateur who agreed to do readings in such circumstances, even in conditions when the sitter was neither seen nor heard. He also enlisted the help of a 'psychic magician' to point out how the mediums involved in the experiments could be cheating in order to create as trick-proof an environment for the experiments as possible.

In the first experiments Schwartz carried out, the average of completely accurate information the mediums gave their unseen sitters was 83%, the sitters only allowed to say Yes or No. This compared with an average of 36% for a control group, which just guessed whether the information they were given about a person was accurate or not. A statistician will tell you the probability of this difference happening by chance alone is less than one in ten million.

To obviate the possibility that the mediums could somehow have found out who the sitters were (information only known to very few people in the experiment) and engaged a private detective to find out information about them, or otherwise discovered details of their lives, another experiment featured ten sitters carefully selected to vary in age, gender and history of departed loved ones, professions, geographical origins and belief in the possibility of survival of the human spirit.

The reading involved not only the medium being unable to see the sitter, but also an initial period of total silence from the sitter, so that the medium had no idea of their gender, age or personality. What's more, each of the sitters was brought into the room in a random order, only decided at the last moment by one of the two experimenters.

Thus, these experiments followed the research mantra of 'replicate and extend' – repeat a procedure that worked in the past and add a new aspect to explore. They still achieved a 70% accuracy of information during the silent period for the mediums.

The striking elements of Schwartz's afterlife experiments are the often highly specific details provided by the mediums, a distinguishing factor from the vague generalised information provided by the fake mediums. For example, all the mediums in separate sittings with one sitter stated that she had a deceased son whose name began with M, that he had died with some kind of explosion (he shot himself), and that he had a small dog with a personality. The chances of this happening are 2.5 billion to one.

Then there was the deceased husband who conveyed the message 'Enjoy the tea' to his wife through one of the mediums. This immediately made sense to the woman. She had never liked tea when her husband was alive but had developed a taste for it later and drank quite a lot of it now. The dead can make humorous comments like this, or insist on a detail the sitter doesn't recognise, but which later turns out to be true when other relatives are consulted.

Another highly specific detail which a medium brought up was the fact that something had been hidden in the sitter's grandmother's carton of Parliament cigarettes. Only his parents knew that her grandson had spiked his grandmother's cigarettes with marijuana to ease her pain. When a control group was asked to guess a brand of cigarettes and what might have been hidden in them, none of them came up with either detail.

On a few occasions, mediums foresaw events which hadn't yet happened, such as, distressingly, the death of a sitter's husband. This suggests that there is an overarching faculty which enables communication with the dead as well as predicting the future; this is a good argument for adopting the notion of psi, which could be a useful cover-all term for what facilitates paranormal activity.

It is interesting that four video cameras which worked perfectly well before and after the afterlife experiments with the mediums didn't work during them. A sitter's Seiko digital watch also started going backwards after apparent communication with his dead father. No jeweller who was consulted could explain the problem. Luckily, audio equipment worked throughout all the experiments.

My own mother could never wear a normal clockwork watch because it always went wrong. This was explained to her as 'having too much electricity' in her hands. I myself used to quite frequently cause a lightbulb filament to break when switching a light on in the old days of such lightbulbs. In the early days of computers, I could also regularly make computers freeze or cause inexplicable failures of programmes. A German physicist I got to know when he came to Canterbury to perfect his English had the same problem, and was even banned from using IT at work.

Thomas Pauli, the physicist who worked on the paranormal with Jung, was famous for causing laboratory equipment to fail; this apparent ability of certain people to cause technical failures is called the Pauli Effect. It seems that some people have a highly developed psi which emits a strong force affecting our modern technology, as well as enabling them to 'tune in' to spirits.

So, what are these 'spirits'? Gordon Smith, a British medium who has written *One Hundred Answers from Spirit*, relaying answers from his spirit guide to his questions, makes a distinction between three entities: a person's spirit, their physical body and their 'emotional body'. Their spirit returns to the spirit world at death, the physical body leaves behind 'a sense of atmosphere' for those in the human world who were attached to it, while the emotional body may be stuck where it died on Earth. 'This leftover residue of that emotional life, if potent enough, can sometimes form a ghostly body, which is no more than a compilation of the more concentrated emotions of its former life.'[16]

Does believing in a soul or spirit which lives on after death preclude accepting the theory of evolution, according to which all biological entities are made up of smaller and simpler parts that constantly combine and separate?

As Hariri points out in *Homo Deus*, the soul cannot be divided or changed, so cannot have come about by natural selection. It is impossible to believe that at some point during our evolution a baby with a soul was born to parents with no soul.

It seems to me the only way to reconcile the two theories is to say that the unicellular organisms from which all life developed had a soul. Perhaps that is not so absurd if we equate the soul with consciousness and accept that all living organisms are conscious. It is worth remembering that Alfred R. Wallace, the co-founder of the theory of evolution with Darwin, was one of the founding members of the Society for Psychical Research in London.

It seems that biologists claim only certain animals have consciousness, so perhaps the clue is there – the soul evolved at a certain point in the development of life on Earth. In 2012, a group of neuroscientists signed the Cambridge Declaration on Consciousness, which 'unequivocally' asserted that 'humans are not unique in possessing the neurological substrates that generate consciousness. Non-human animals, including all mammals and birds, and many other creatures, including octopuses, also

---

16.   pp. 57-8

possess these neural substrates.'[17]

Buddhism, and philosophers like Sam Harris who aspire to spirituality without religion, claim that we have no self (*anattā* or *anātman*), no individual unchanging soul. But my friend's and my experience of the spirits of dead relatives around us belies this. Clearly, each human being must have a separate 'soul' or 'self' if this lives on after death.

Let me return to the kitchen tap turning full on of its own accord. Was this my father's spirit a little delayed in going to the spirit world, or was it his 'emotional body'? Or was it a poltergeist formed by me or Jana? Popular understanding of poltergeists is that a disturbed adolescent girl can actually cause objects to move through psychokinesis, the subconscious power of the mind.

On the other hand, the medium Gordon Smith says 'a poltergeist is literally a noisy ghost emitting energy from the unsettled human who is hiding, deep within them, the fear and angst which is not being recognised by those around them – built-up frustration, anger, jealousy or maybe even hatred causes poltergeists – it isn't the same as a ghost, which is the leftover emotional body or stain from a distressed human life.'

While working on this book, I had another experience which most would call that of a poltergeist. There were no teenage girls present. On Tuesday afternoons I volunteer in my local Oxfam Bookshop and in September was delighted to see some-one had donated a large number of back copies of the Journal of the Society for Psychical Research.

I managed to look through them one afternoon, selecting

---

17.   *Andrews, p. 51*

ones to buy which had articles of interest for my research. Of course, I would periodically pause in this reading to serve customers. While I was serving one customer, a small brown hardback literally shot off a shelf to my left where hardbacks of no particular subject are kept. There was no one anywhere near it and the way it came off the shelf couldn't have been the result of it having simply fallen off because it had been badly put back. The woman I was serving and I looked at the book in astonishment and I said 'Ah! We have a poltergeist!' and we both laughed.

When she had left the shop, I went over to pick the book up. It was entitled *Hints and Observations for those Investigating the Phenomenon of Spiritualism* by W.J.Crawford. It had been published in New York in 1918 and the title page declared it was 'A record of the series of scientific tests carried out by the author in 1915 and 1916 to determine the amount, direction and nature of the force used in levitation, and other Psychic Phenomena'. The author was a lecturer in Mechanical Engineering at the Queen's University of Belfast.

The only conclusion I could come to was that a helpful spirit had drawn the book to my attention as I never normally looked at that shelf. It certainly wasn't a section where you'd expect to find such a book.

It would appear that there is incontrovertible evidence that we are surrounded by the spirits of the dead and that they watch over our lives, disconcerting as that observation is.

But when you think how much is invisible and inaudible to us, it becomes more plausible.

Ultrasound equipment is commonplace in medical examination nowadays. It apparently produces as loud a sound as an underground train coming into a station, around 100 decibels, but human beings are completely oblivious to all this racket going on around us.

Bats make a high-pitched sound we can't hear but is at 140 decibels – the sound of a rock concert – 15 decibels above our pain level.

And then there is the 'dark energy', which physicists posit must permeate almost 70% of the universe, although they can say little about it. It is tempting, to say the least, to identify it with the channel by which the dead can communicate with the living, move objects and pass through time and space as if they don't exist.

Or is it better to think of spirits existing in another 'dimension'? Physicists posit anything from five to eleven dimensions – does one of them contain the spirits of the dead?

Quantum mechanics posits the existence of multiple parallel universes and physicists believe that interaction can take place between them. This could be in the form of voices heard by mediums or forces moving objects.

Has literature from *The Odyssey* to Philip Pullman's *His Dark Materials* trilogy tapped into a physical reality with the idea of an underworld, which living human beings can only visit at their peril?

10.

That strange feeling: 1998/2003/2015

Premonition, precognition and entanglement again

Extraordinary claims require extraordinary evidence.

Carl Sagan

The years of focussing on one day at a time and not thinking too much about our lives had gone on throughout the Nineties. By 1998 Goran had decided to resign as Professor of Playwriting at the Faculty of Dramatic Arts in Skopje, but he didn't come to live and work in Canterbury. Through the Swedish contacts he had developed during his work with Chris Torch on productions for Cultural City of Europe festivals, he took up an invitation to be a Visiting Professor at the Drama Institute in Stockholm.

Two years of commuting between the Swedish capital and Canterbury replaced the six years of commuting between the Macedonian capital and Canterbury. It was in Stockholm that Goran wrote and had published his playwriting tool for students: *A Little Book of Traps*, which has received high praise from specialists.

I still didn't feel at home in England as I had felt in Skopje. When I had a week off for my fiftieth birthday in 1999, I took Goran on a tour of all the places I had lived or had a connection with in England. I was trying to regain the past I had lived in this country, reminding myself that I did belong here, that I was, after all, English.

We went to Great Offley in Hertfordshire where the family vault was and where I had scattered my Great Auntie May's ashes with my father on a beautiful summer's day which stood out in my memory as archetypally English – a village churchyard, a thirteenth-century church, a feeling of calm and continuity, of peace.

We drove on into the Midlands, to Leicester. My childhood home on Highway Road was now in the middle of an area where the only people we saw on the streets were women in burqas with their children. The golf course practice ground at the end of the garden had been built on, and the grocer's, the chemist's and the barber's in Allandale Road, all of which had often been visited on a Saturday morning shopping trip, had all gone.

But, seven years after I had come back to live in England, I did begin to feel some connection with the child who had grown up in this country, with the young woman who had gone to university in Bristol, worked in London and studied in Wales.

The following year, Goran finally settled in Canterbury. We would keep Macedonia for holidays and he would take up offers of work at the University of Kent teaching playwriting and then at Christ Church – a university college at the time – teaching screenwriting in the Film, TV and Radio Department, where he was soon given a permanent job. We all got into a rhythm of returning to Skopje at least once a year to see friends and family.

Ig was seventeen and had recently passed his driving test when there was another weird moment in my life. He had the use of our car – the one Dad had given me because he couldn't change gear properly – and would often use it to drive to school.

As always, my job teaching English to business people meant I had to get up early every day to be at work by 8.30am at the latest and would leave the house before anyone else. One day I felt absolutely terrible at breakfast. Not a physical problem, but something affecting my mood dramatically. I felt as if a heavy black cloud was hanging over my head, as if life was suddenly empty and meaningless, not worth living. This was really so unlike me that Goran noticed and asked me what the matter was. I told him I felt something awful was going to happen and I couldn't stand the feeling. He was unsympathetic.

'Time to go to work,' he commented, 'you'll feel better when you've got something else to occupy you.'

I dragged myself to work and by break-time at 10.15 the cloud had indeed lifted and I was feeling myself again. I thought no more about it, but when I got home that afternoon at 5.30, Goran was looking pale and greeted me quietly.

'Sit down,' he said, 'I've got something to tell you. But don't worry, everything's all right now. It's just we've had a bit of a shock.'

I sat down. Goran told me how Ig had picked up his friend Chris that morning from his house on the other side of Canterbury. They were driving down the hill into town when a little boy on a scooter suddenly shot across the road. Ig swerved and slammed the brakes on but heard a sickening thud as something hit the car.

For a brief moment, he was convinced he had killed the little boy, who must be lying dead in the road, but then he glimpsed him running through the front gate of a house just down the road. He quickly parked the car, and he and Chris ran up to the house and knocked on the door. A man opened the door.

'Your little boy,' began Ig, 'is he, … is he OK?'

'What's he been doing?' asked the man.

Ig haltingly explained what had happened. The man got very angry.

'I've told him before!' he shouted. 'That's the second time he's crossed the road on that scooter. He'll get himself killed. Is your car damaged? Are you all right?'

Ig was by now shaking from the shock he'd experienced. The man walked down to the car with him and they noted the dent in the front wing where the scooter had banged into it. The man gave Ig his name and phone number and told him he would cover the cost of repair.

Somehow Ig drove home and luckily Goran was there. They called a doctor, who told Ig to go to bed and rest. He was still there when I came home in the evening. It didn't take me long to remember the unprecedented feeling I had had in the morning and to recognise that it must have been a premonition of the accident about to happen, which was to shake my son so badly.

During our trip round Latin America five years later, I had another strong premonition. Ig and I were staying at the Casa Gonzalez in Mexico City and preparing to set off for the pyramids of Teotihuacan.

I had a sudden urge to know what was going on in Iraq. It was 9th April 2003 and the so-called coalition troops from the

USA and the UK had invaded Iraq three weeks before, ostensibly to find and destroy the weapons of mass destruction which the President, Saddam Hussein, was allegedly hiding from the weapons inspectors.

I had hardly given a second thought to this invasion since arriving in Mexico but, that morning, something made me eager to know what was going on. I asked our kind host and other guests at the breakfast table if they'd heard any news; nobody knew anything, but several expressed an interest, especially the Americans there.

Our host took us into the sitting room and turned on the television. When the picture appeared, it was of the statue of Saddam Hussein in Baghdad being pulled down by an American vehicle in front of a baying crowd. That was to turn out to be the iconic image of the whole war, and we witnessed it on TV as it happened on the other side of the world.

Strangely enough, the same kind of coincidence was to happen in 2015, again in Mexico. This time Ig had a wife and daughter with us and we were in the Yucatan, touring the great Mayan sites. It was 2nd December.

I knew there was to be a debate in the House of Commons on allowing airstrikes against ISIL in Syria that day, but I had no idea when. It was late afternoon and it suddenly came into my head to go to the BBC News website, something I rarely do when abroad – I normally only use my little netbook for checking my emails.

As the website came up, there was live coverage from the House. The tellers were just announcing the results of the vote to the Speaker: the Ayes to the right 397, the Noes to the left 223. The debate had apparently gone on all day but I had gone online at the exact moment when the voting data were being reported.

∾

All these premonitions can't really be put down to coincidence. But to explore them, we are required to take on Keats's famous Negative Capability, 'capable of being in uncertainties, mysteries, doubts, without any irritable reaching after fact and reason.' I love that word 'irritable' – it captures so well that feeling we have – 'There must be a rational explanation for this!' It's very difficult to suspend the usual critical, analytical reasoning and to go on exploring what's going on.

This takes us back to entanglement, which we touched on in Chapter 7 when examining inception. Einstein famously called it 'spooky action at a distance' and didn't want to accept that it was happening.

Entanglement was first considered just an abstract theoretical concept, a hiccup occurring for a brief instant only in the realm of atoms. By 2004, however, research into it had developed to such an extent that *New Scientist* writer Michael Brooks would write: 'Physicists now believe that entanglement between particles exists everywhere, all the time, and have recently found shocking evidence that it affects the wider, 'macroscopic' world that we inhabit.'[18] It has even been suggested by physicist Johann Summhammer from the Vienna University of Technology that [entanglement] 'could coordinate the behaviour of members of a species, because it is independent of

---

18.   Brooks, M. (March 27, 2004) 'The weirdest link', *New Scientist*

distance and requires no physical link.'[19]

In 1959 Czech physician Štěpán Figar carried out a fascinating experiment with a pair of isolated people who were completely unaware of each other and of the nature of the experiment. They were each attached to a plethysmograph, which measures peripheral blood volume. When one was given mental arithmetic exercises to do, the blood pressure of the other person changed significantly. Psychiatrist D. J. West independently corroborated Figar's analysis of the data as demonstrating telepathy between the two people.

In 1963 Russian physiologist Leonid Vasiliev published *Experiments in Mental Suggestion*, reporting on experiments where somnambulists could be given hypnotic suggestions from a considerable distance, sometimes thousands of miles away, to fall into a deep trance. These and other experiments carried out in the Soviet Union were taken very seriously, both by the scientific community and at the highest levels of government. Both Soviet and American scientists conducted extensive research into 'remote viewing' during the Cold War, attempting to spy on each other at a distance using subjects with high levels of extrasensory perception.

My premonition of Ig's accident is actually very similar to the event which triggered the exploration of psi by Hans Berger, a German psychiatrist known as the inventor of electroencephalography (EEG), a method for recording brain waves.

In the early 1890s, Berger was doing training as a cavalry officer when his horse suddenly reared and he fell onto the road

---

19.   Summhammer, J. (March 15, 2005) 'Quantum Cooperation of Two Insects', arXiv:quant-ph/0503136v2, Cornell University. Online at https://arxiv.org/abs/quant-ph/0503136

into the path of a horse-drawn cannon. He realised in horror that he was about to be crushed to death but, fortunately for him, the driver of the battery managed to stop the horses before they reached Berger lying in the road.

However, back home his elder sister, who he was very close to, had a terrible premonition that something had happened to Hans and she persuaded her father to send him a telegram. Berger was concerned to receive a telegram from his father but, on reading the content, realised that he must somehow have communicated his terror earlier in the day to his sister. Or perhaps she had a premonition of his alarm as I did with my son.

Hans Berger went on to study medicine with a focus on understanding how 'psychic energy', as he called it, could transmit a message to someone miles away. Years later, in 1924, he developed a method of recording what were first called 'Berger rhythms' after him. These signals are now known as electroencephalograms or EEGs. He had established that electrical activity of the human brain correlated with different subjective states of mind.

In 1965 the Department of Opthalmology at Jefferson Medical College in Philadelphia had a paper published in the prestigious mainstream journal *Science*, which demonstrated astonishing correspondences in the electrocephalographs of pairs of identical twins when isolated at a distance. The idea that minds could be entangled was born.

Parapsychologists and others put precognition down to psi, the unknown element in any form of extrasensory perception. As mentioned earlier, psi doesn't appear to be an electromagnetic force as it still works in metal chambers, Faraday cages and deep in the earth; what's more, it isn't blocked by intervening material bodies or fields. It therefore doesn't follow the curvature of the earth like radio waves. In cases of telepathy and telekinesis, it was clear that psi is unlimited by space and time. With precognition, it appears psi also violates physical causality: information about an event is gained before the event occurs.

Some scientists claim to have found scientific evidence for premonitions with odds against chance of an astonishing 125,000 to 1 for experiments in the mid-1990s by Dean Radin and his colleagues in the USA. They consisted of measuring a physical reaction in the skin three or four seconds *before* an emotional picture was shown. These experiments have been rubbished by the scientific community, who see any number of flaws in the methodology.

Experiments in the 1930s, however, at the pioneering Parapsychological Laboratory at Duke University, North Carolina, showed people could say which of five cards with different symbols had been turned over by someone in another room with a far greater degree of accuracy than statistical probability would predict. This also seems to be linked to precognition – some subjects were actually predicting what the next card would be before it was even seen by the 'agent'.

Extensive investigation of these experiments by an independent researcher found that the results did decline slightly as controls against potential problems such as sensory cues, recording errors and experimenter fraud were improved, but even the most highly controlled studies emerged with odds against chance of a staggering 375 *trillion* to 1.

It seems, however, that we don't set much store by what statistics tell us. A key factor in the premonition people experience in everyday life, rather than in a scientist's lab, is a strong emotional tie to the person experiencing the event, as in the case of my ghastly feeling an hour before Ig's accident, or an emotional link to the event. I was fervently against the invasion of Iraq and British involvement in the Syrian War, so it would make sense that news concerning these two issues would affect my consciousness.

On the other hand, I have never had a premonition to turn on the TV because some football team is about to score a decisive goal. I'm simply not interested in any sport.

What I conclude here is that it is unlikely that scientific experiments can give us convincing proof of premonition because it happens when there is strong personal involvement in an event about to happen. This is different from the kind of response we have to images of atrocities or starving children, however strong those reactions may be. And, in the nature of things, we don't know when these premonitions are going to happen in order to be able to measure them scientifically.

Nevertheless, there is a kind of precognition which is more like prophecy and doesn't involve such intense emotion. Sci fi author Philip K. Dick of *Blade Runner* fame had many unusual experiences in his writing career. According to the consciousness theorist, Anthony Peake[20], 'Phil stated many times that his earlier novels were based upon events that happened later in his life. He believed that he was drawing up his inspiration from future memory.' Dick is said to have had a sense of another

20. Anthony Peake (2013) *A life of Philip K. Dick: The Man Who Remembered the Future*, Arcturus Publishing

consciousness accompanying him from an early age, something like a higher self or daemon[21], which provided him with his intuitions and premonitions.

It is seventeen years since Rupert Sheldrake wrote in his Introduction to *The Sense of Being Stared At* that 'the boundaries of scientific 'normality' are shifting again with a dawning recognition of the reality of consciousness. The powers of the mind, hitherto ignored by physics, are the new scientific frontier.'

---

21.   See p. 25 of this book

11.

I don't want to go on living: 2015-2017

Mind over Matter, Death Bed Visions

There were some very important friends in Skopje who were not Macedonians. They were Graham and Peggy Reid. Graham had been the British lector in Skopje before me for eight years and Peggy had joined him there after they married in 1969. Peggy had been one of Goran's teachers when he was a student of English, and he had spent many an evening at their house in Skopje during his studies. He had come to look on Graham as a kind of guru, a wise mentor. Both Graham and Peggy were poets, although they never publicised or published their writing. They had met while reading English at Cambridge.

When I arrived in Skopje in 1974, Graham and Peggy had returned to the UK. The University had been without a lector for a year, but Graham and Peggy had not been forgotten. When discussing the courses I was teaching in language, translation or literature, I would often be met with the comment: 'That's not how Graham / Peggy did it.' I came to resent them both immeasurably before I met them.

When I did, it was the following summer and I was with Goran, their devoted protégé. It didn't take me long to fall under their spell as so many had before me. Their warm and friendly welcome was combined with easy conversation and a genuine interest in their guests and open hospitality. Every year we would always spend some time with Graham and Peggy, wherever they were in England. Towards the end of their careers, they came back to Skopje to teach English and for a few short years we were colleagues.

Our lives were so similar – the people we knew and loved, the jobs we did, the two countries we lived in. When it came to appointing guardians in our will for our two children, Graham and Peggy were the ones we chose, the only people who shared so much of what we held dear, whether it was friends, beliefs or cultural values. Not that we didn't both love our brothers, but neither of them shared our two cultures as Peggy and Graham did. With our friends, we knew our children would have been brought up as we would have done. It never came to that, of course – our children have both grown up, moved away and started families of their own. But for them, Peggy and Graham had become replacement grandparents, our children's real ones all having died before they were born or when they were little.

When the children and I returned to England in 1992 with the Yugoslav wars creeping down the country, Graham and Peggy stayed on and would come and see us when they came to the UK for their holidays. But by the time Goran had joined us in Canterbury, they had grown tired of using the house in Radstock, where Peggy had grown up, as their base – they knew few people there. They asked us to put them in touch with estate agents in Canterbury so they could sell their house in Radstock and buy a house near us.

A week after they made this request, I happened to come out of my front door to see the estate agent who sold us our house taking photographs of No.17 next door. That evening I went to see Dave and Denise, who lived there, and asked if they were selling up. They were – going to New Zealand where Dave had grown up. I then emailed Graham and Peggy to see if they would like to be our next-door neighbours, or whether that might be a bit too close for comfort. They were delighted at the opportunity and dealt with Dave and Denise directly, paying the asking price. The house never went on the market. Another strange 'coincidence'.

No.17 became a house where we could put up friends who came to stay, just as Graham and Peggy used our flat in Skopje. Then came some of the happiest years of my life when they retired and came to live next door. Our gardens were divided by a fence which ended at the path behind our houses, where we could wheel our bins along and up the passage to the street for collection. There was no gate between us.

We would often join each other in our gardens for coffee when they were outside, or knock on each other's back door to see if they wanted a cup of tea and a chat. The chats usually turned into a long debate on practically any subject under the sun, often prompted by a programme on BBC Radio Four, which Peggy listened to every day for most of the day, her portable radio and earphones attached when doing the gardening. I came to look on Peggy as the sister I never had.

Graham wasn't happy, however. He was, in fact, clinically depressed and having to take pills to deal with the problem. I was devastated when Graham persuaded Peggy to move to Scotland a few years later to be near his sister, Jenny. They started looking for a house in Edinburgh near her and her husband, Andrew, a couple we knew well from their visits to Macedonia and Canterbury. In the end, they had an extension built on Jenny and Andrew's house and moved in there.

Graham had felt a need to go back to his roots; perhaps, subconsciously, he wanted to go home to die. It was the following year when he discovered he had lung cancer. He died in March and we couldn't attend the funeral as we were in Skopje for Easter, but at least we could be present at the commemoration held by the English Department for him in the university amphitheatre, when colleague after colleague spoke of their happy memories of the Scotsman who had felt most at home in Macedonia. One of them read Graham's translation of the most famous Macedonian poem, *Longing for the South*.

Sad as I was at Graham's death, there was a part of me which now hoped Peggy might come back to Canterbury to live, and I would have her nearby again.

I hadn't realised how much Peggy was one half of a remarkable couple, a symbiotic relationship which meant that she had no wish to go on living without her other half, without Graham. Graham and Peggy, Peggy and Graham – there was rarely a case when their names were not mentioned together. And as one of her Macedonian students put it, 'the bird cannot fly with one wing'. It was symbolic of their relationship that, though they were both heavy smokers, they only ever seemed to have one pack of cigarettes between them, only one lighter. They behaved in so many ways as if they were one person in two bodies. Peggy talked about 'this ideal relationship which needs no words' and she regretted that she had never said thank you to Graham for having made her happy.

Peggy had had breast cancer ten years earlier and was still having regular annual check-ups. She had had the all-clear in September. Now, less than six months later, she learnt that the lump she had developed on her back was cancerous and inoperable and her body was riddled with the disease; only palliative care could be offered.

She greeted the fact with relief, for it meant that she wouldn't have to face life without Graham for very long, that her grief would be short-lived. I spent days with her in Edinburgh twice over the next few months. There was no denying she was looking forward to death. Her only concern was that it shouldn't be too painful. Although she wasn't religious, she seemed to feel in some way she would be joining Graham. Indeed, a few hours before she died, the nurse with her reported that she smiled and was full of joy. When asked why she was smiling, Peggy replied:

'I can see Graham.'

I have absolutely no doubt that Peggy willed herself to have cancer. It sounds shocking, but everything about this case convinced me that, if a person decides they no longer wish to go on living, they can somehow give themselves a terminal illness. Peggy was to die five months after Graham.

There is a flip side to this, of course. Experiments have apparently shown that people who visualise their cancers shrinking have much better recovery results than those who don't.

Then there is the case of a friend of mine who is subject to migraines from time to time. She doesn't like taking painkillers and prefers to let the attack take its course, feeling it is somehow cleaning her out from inside. Once during the worst of an attack, she actually managed to go to sleep, something unheard of before. She dreamt she was sitting in a lotus position, a turban on her head. Slowly she started levitating and had the most wonderful feeling of joy and liberation. She woke up and all trace of the migraine had gone. Sadly, this has only ever happened once, but it is a clear instance of being able to cure oneself through the power of the mind.

 co

I appreciate I am on very delicate ground when talking about people being able to make themselves ill, or cure themselves simply through the power of their minds. However, I can't forget my own experience not so long ago.

My brother Richard had a heart attack in the night, though he wasn't too sure what had happened to him. He went to the doctor's, who sent him straight to hospital and it was soon established that he needed a very serious operation to do a complete heart bypass. I went to see him in intensive care and was very concerned at how ill he looked. Not long afterwards, he had to be opened up again and it was a long recovery. We were all very shaken by his experience.

Not long after my brother's operation, I talked to my own doctor, who thought I should see a specialist as my genetic risk was very high: angina ran in my mother's family with my grandfather, uncle and mother all dying of heart attacks. The specialist decided he would do an angiogram to check the state of my arteries and an appointment was made at Margate Hospital to do it in a fortnight's time.

While waiting, I started getting a racing heartbeat, especially at night, and this culminated in a full-scale episode at work one lunchtime. I was rushed up to the hospital in Canterbury and was kept in overnight.

When the day of the angiogram came and Goran and I went to Margate, I was already convinced that the consultant would find I had inherited my mother's heart disease, like my brother. I went through the procedure and lay in bed waiting fatalistically for the consultant to tell me the bad news.

In fact, he turned up smiling and told me my arteries were clear and I had no signs of heart disease. It turned out my episodes had been panic attacks, entirely caused by my own fears. I had never experienced them before my brother's heart attack and I have never experienced them since I was given the all-clear.

So, I know from experience that people are quite capable of subconsciously causing their own health problems.

Interestingly, it turns out that 'placebo effects and related kinds of psychosomatic phenomena ... have long been informally recognized and are now widely accepted, but only because it was thought possible to find physical explanations for them.'[22] These, such as the interaction of the central nervous and immune systems, have not proved satisfactory, however, even for the placebo effect. They fail to explain many similar phenomena.

Recently, I read an edited extract of Johann Hari's book *Lost Connections* about depression and its treatment. He asserts that the story sufferers have been told for 35 years that depression is caused by a spontaneous imbalance of chemicals in the brain is untrue. He draws the parallel with those who are grieving for a loved one: they display exactly the same symptoms as those with depression. There even used to be a 'grief exception' for US doctors diagnosing depression according to a patient's symptoms: in a situation of grieving, such symptoms were said to be natural.

22. Kelly

But doctors soon realised there was a problem here: how could the same symptoms be said to have natural causes in one case and not in the other? The 'grief exception' was removed, and everyone suffering the symptoms of depression was treated with the same drugs. However, most of them found they were not cured and their mental anguish soon returned.

Johann Hari went on a journey round the world to meet people everywhere suffering from depression. 'They taught me,' he says, 'that it [depression] is not what we have been told it is up to now. I found there is evidence that seven specific factors in the way we are living today are causing depression and anxiety to rise – alongside two real biological factors (such as your genes) that can combine with these forces to make it worse.'

Hari claims the cure for depression lies in finding a way to solve the problem that is causing the depression in the first place. 'If you are depressed and anxious, you are not a machine with malfunctioning parts. You are a human being with unmet needs. The only real way out of our epidemic of despair is for all of us, together, to begin to meet those human needs – for deep connection, to the things that really matter in life.'

So, people with depression appear to hold the key to their mental health in their own hands.

As a corollary to this, I should add that a study that came out in February 2018, after Hari's book, concludes that anti-depressant drugs do work, although some are more effective than others; Amitriptyline is significantly better than Fluoxetine (Prozac), for example.

In April 2018, Edward Bullmore, Professor of Psychiatry at Cambridge University, published *The Inflamed Mind*, a radical new approach to mental disorders which claims that they have their roots in the immune system for many people.

Medical experts are beginning to realise that the mind is very much linked to the body and that this link can work both ways. People with chronic physical illnesses often develop depression; if a person has one heart attack and becomes depressed, they are much more likely to have a second one.

A holistic approach to all disease is required, whether physical or mental. This is advocated by King's Health Partners in London, which has outpatient centres with both a physician and a psychologist examining patients; they recognise that the link between mind and body can be key in health issues.

It seems medical opinion is returning to the view already held by some philosophers in Ancient Times: treatment for depression involves the whole body – a change of scenery, rest, a good diet and exercise.[23]

To return to Peggy, I attributed her 'vision' of her husband Graham shortly before she died to the strong drugs she was on to help her die as painlessly as possible. It turns out that these Death Bed Visions (DBVs) are not a rare phenomenon. Like Near Death Experiences (NDEs), they are reported all over the world and are remarkably similar across all cultures.

Research was published in 1977 by Doctors Karlis Osis and Erlendur Haraldsson in their book *At the Hour of Death*, which covered thousands of surveys of doctors, nurses and health care workers dealing with the dying over more than a decade. This showed that a dying person often reports that a dead relative or friend is coming to take them away, and is taken over by a feeling of great elation. Even those in pain or deep depression

---

23. Amy Liptrot speaking on BBC Radio Four Start The Week programme on 8th March 2021 about her book, *The New Anatomy of Melancholy*

143

are momentarily relieved of these during their vision.

Another remarkable element DBVs have in common is that the dying person is completely aware of their surroundings and treat what they see as part of the normal physical reality of the situation. Moreover, their visions follow the same model whether they are believers or non-believers.

We should also note that William Barrett, a Professor of Physics at the Royal College of Science in Dublin, who carried out a study on this as long ago as 1926, noticed two features which suggest people may well be experiencing a real event.

First, some of those dying saw relatives or friends coming to take them who they didn't know were dead, communications in the Twenties taking much longer than they do today. In all cases, it later emerged that these people had in fact died before the DBVs recorded.

The second corroborating fact was that children quite often expressed surprise that the 'angel' they saw coming to take them away didn't have wings. If they were hallucinating, surely they would imagine a vision close to their image of an angel with big white wings...

AFTERWORD

The day science begins to study non-physical phenomena, it will make more progress in one decade than in all the previous centuries of its existence.

NIKOLA TESLA

If you wish to upset the law that all crows are black, you mustn't seek to show that no crows are; it is enough if you prove one single crow to be white.

WILLIAM JAMES, AMERICAN PSYCHOLOGIST AND PHILOSOPHER

(1842-1910)

We shall not cease from exploration
And the end of our exploring
Will be to arrive where we started
And know the place for the first time.

T.S.ELIOT – *FOUR QUARTETS* 'LITTLE GIDDING'

While I was sitting on our sofa thinking about writing this book, my husband Goran called our son Igor on his mobile phone. Ig is living in Montenegro at the moment.

I watched Goran talking to Ig and suddenly saw what was happening from a completely different perspective. How incredible was it that someone could hold a thin piece of metal and plastic to their ear and actually have a conversation with someone else more than a thousand miles away! We don't bat an eyelid that someone can be actually communicating with someone at a huge distance, hearing them as well as if they're in the same room, simply through the medium of that small instrument; we have grown up with telephones, followed how the technology has developed and taken it completely for granted. We don't even have to know it all depends on invisible radio waves.

So how many other invisible waves or forces or forms of energy might be out there, which we simply don't yet know about? After all, it's only just over 150 years since James Clerk Maxwell mathematically predicted the existence of radio waves. It took another twenty years before Heinrich Hertz produced them in the laboratory.

Dark matter and dark energy are thought to exist in order to reconcile the measured geometry of space with the total amount of matter in the universe, and yet they have never been observed.

The experiences I have recounted and examined in this book are persuasive that human beings have some kind of psychic powers which can wordlessly and instantly communicate with others, regardless of distance. The use of the term 'psi' for this seems to me very useful. It covers not only the way I felt my mother's pain in hospital in England thousands of miles away in Finland, but also my precognition of my son's near accident, the way people are drawn to each other in amazing instances of coincidence and inception.

I tend to think that psi can also be used to cover what British philosopher Gilbert Ryle called 'the Ghost in the Machine' – our consciousness, our soul, our spirit, what the modern development of ancient Vedic traditions would call our 'astral energy body',[24] the part of us which has an afterlife and which communicates with the spirits of the dead, as well as of the living.

Uncomfortable as some may find it, it seems from the evidence I have produced in this book that there are invisible spirits around us observing what we do, and sometimes seeking out ways of communicating with us.

It's difficult at my time of life to change my intellectual way of viewing the world and my tendency not to believe anything unless I can see it. Of course, this is a nice contradiction: I can't see radio waves but I know they're there and I take advantage of their existence every day in a variety of ways. And what about that microwave which heats up food in a matter of seconds, as if by magic? I suppose what I'm saying is that most of us need the scientists to tell us something exists and for them to make use of it in visible ways before it becomes something we accept as an ordinary part of our lives.

On the other hand, it seems clear that the scientific method of 'systematic observation, measurement, and experiment, and the formulation, testing, and modification of hypotheses' (Oxford English Dictionary) is not going to be appropriate in much of the field of the supernatural.

As noted throughout this book, the experiences I and others close to me have had have all occurred in unpredictable circumstances (death, prophetic dreams, telepathy, premonition, precognition, coincidence) or moments of extreme pain or high emotion (pain telepathy, bilocation). Thus, they never lend themselves to observation, measurement or experiment, which

---

24. Adams Media (2017) p.41

require planning and preparation. As Beichler notes, 'science will never accept the reality of psi based upon experimental 'proofs' of its existence, especially when these proofs are statistical in nature', as are the results on extrasensory perception.

Evolutionary biologist Richard Dawkins, the University of Oxford's Professor for Public Understanding of Science from 1995 until 2008, is also reluctant to use the word 'supernatural'. Many of us will wholeheartedly agree with him that 'if there is something that appears to lie beyond the natural world as it is now imperfectly understood, we hope eventually to understand it and embrace it within the natural.'

Plato's cave allegory in *The Republic* is clearly a useful image here. Plato pictured captives chained up in a cave so that they could only see the back wall. The only things they see in their lives are the shadows of objects passed in front of a fire behind them, to which they give names. If they are freed from the cave and go out into the world, they have no way of expressing the reality of what they see. This is the problem of physicists or anyone else trying to describe the invisible world around us, which, it appears, must be made up of other dimensions where the spirits of the dead move and interact.

In August 2018 I was coming to a dead end with this book after having had it rejected by a variety of agents, who all said it was fascinating but not commercial. They couldn't sell it. Perhaps if I had been a celebrity, it would have been a different matter.

We had had a lovely summer holiday in Northern Greece and then my husband Goran had gone off to Skopje for the month of August to write a new TV series for young people on the Macedonian language, a follow-up to the one he had created with his old friend Slobodan Unkovski to teach children the alphabet.

That was the second year we had been apart in August. I had discovered that I couldn't take extreme heat anymore – I went dizzy and nauseous when the temperatures rose above 40. Having been brought up with such heat from birth, it didn't bother Goran. On the contrary, he took pleasure in sweating away in the flat with the blinds down and huge watermelons in the fridge to be cut and wallowed in at frequent intervals.

I took the opportunity of getting the living room of our English home redecorated the first year we were apart, and then having double glazed windows and laminate doors installed in 2018. My evenings were spent reading episodes of the TV series Goran was writing and sending to me at regular intervals.

When he came back in September, Goran seemed very tired. He began falling asleep at all times of the day and having a lie-in every day. He put it down to the fact that he'd worked so hard in Skopje and actually completed 15 episodes of the series.

When this pattern continued after the first week, however, I started having thoughts of our friend Ronnie Wathen, the wonderfully eccentric third son of an earl, a poet who took his Irish pipes everywhere and played them with gusto. He had come to visit us with his lovely Icelandic artist wife, Åsta Kristinsdottir, in our rented house in Canterbury shortly after we had moved from Skopje. Ronnie wasn't even 60 that year but he fell asleep in his armchair after lunch. When he woke up, we all made jibes about him being an old man now, who needed to nap in the afternoon. Three months later, he died from a brain tumour.

I went to see my friend Mira, the doctor. We had coffee

together and I told her of my fears. 'Oh no, don't worry,' she said. 'If he doesn't have headaches, it's very unlikely to be a brain tumour.'

The days went by and Goran started having odd moments of confusion, absence or forgetfulness. Mira now gave me a long list of things to look out for and I was well aware she thought he might be in the early stages of dementia.

I finally got him to see a doctor in October, but he told her that he was simply tired of living in two homes, with two languages and two cultures. She gave him a form to take for blood tests but he refused to get them done, still saying there was nothing wrong with him.

It was at the end of the month that his colleagues finally persuaded him he wasn't himself and he should have time off to sort it out. The blood tests he finally did were all fine and it was only the MRI on 9th November which showed up a brain tumour. It was inoperable, but they were going to do a biopsy to see if it was malignant or not.

Goran was still eating normally and getting up every day, but quickly tiring. We got a wheelchair when we went out anywhere. On the 21st, he woke up and could neither eat, drink nor move. We called an ambulance and one of the paramedics finally persuaded him to go to hospital. The CT scan that evening showed the tumour had started bleeding and that was the beginning of the end. No biopsy was possible.

He died on the 27th.

They had made him comfortable and I don't believe he had any real pain at any point. He had a lovely private room next to a quadrangle full of trees and bushes, where the birds came to roost every evening and sang every morning.

When I write this, it's as if I'm writing about a dream I had. I'm still expecting him to come home at any moment, even though I watched him die and arranged his funeral. It's a very strange state to be in. As I sat alone with him in his bamboo coffin in the room at the undertaker's, I decided to see if he would give me proof he was still around in some invisible form.

'If you're in an afterlife and happy, please give me a sign,' I said.

That evening, my son-in-law Matt and I were in the dining room after dinner with Jana and Ig upstairs. All of a sudden, there was an almighty crash from the kitchen next door.

We got up to investigate but could see nothing untoward. We went on into the bathroom. There we found the shower curtain collapsed on the floor. It was attached to a long metal bar on a spring, which could hardly slip off the wall of its own accord. It had also been right up against the ceiling, where no one but six-foot-two Goran could have reached it. I had my proof.

So now I am able to do what Rumi advises: 'Sell your cleverness and buy bewilderment.'

I now find my questioning is at an end. I no longer seek an explanation for all the supernatural phenomena I have experienced. I no longer yearn for some brilliant quantum physicist to propose a ground-breaking theory which will reveal what consciousness is, how it lives on after death, how it can communicate with the living and amongst the living.

I have been given illustrations of the existence of a much vaster physical reality than can normally be accounted for by scientists.

But I am a mere human being. I can never understand what

I am actually a part of. Perhaps no human being ever can.

For me, it is finally enough to wonder at the marvels of Nature, even when others call them supernatural. I don't need a religion to follow or a god to worship. I have simply amended my philosophy of life to take in the reality of phenomena which defy explanation, and accepted that they probably always will.

Now I understand that Zen saying:

Before Enlightenment, chop wood, carry water.

After Enlightenment, chop wood, carry water.

BIBLIOGRAPHY

Adams Media (2017) *The Supernatural Guide to the Other Side*, Simon & Schuster Inc.

Andrews, K. (2014) *The Animal Mind: An Introduction to the Philosophy of Animal Cognition*, Taylor & Francis

Beichler, James E. (2008) *To Die For: The Physical Reality of Conscious Survival,* Trafford Publishing

Beichler, James E. (2017) *Paraphysical Principles of Natural Philosophy,* LAP LAMBERT Academic Publishing (PhD dissertation from 1999)

Bowie, Fiona (2011) *Tales from the Afterlife*, O-Books, John Hunt Publishing Ltd, Hants

Capra, Fritjof (1982) *The Tao of Physics: an Exploration of the Parallels between Modern Physics and Eastern Mysticism*, Flamingo

Cardeña, Etzel, John Palmer and David Marcusson-Clavertz ed. (2015) *Parapsychology: a handbook for the 21st century*, Jefferson, North Carolina: McFarland & Company, Inc., Publishers

Carroll, Sean, interview on www.wired.com/2010/02/what-is-time/

Carson S. H. (2003) with Peterson J.B. & Higgins D.M. 'Decreased latent inhibition is associated with increased creative achievement in high-functioning individuals', J Pers Soc Psychol. 2003 Sep;85(3):499-506 (Abstract)

Carter, Christopher David (2012) *Science and the Afterlife Experience: Evidence for the Immortality of Consciousness*, Inner Traditions

Clarke, Roger (2012) *A Natural History of Ghosts: 500 Years of Hunting for Proof,* Penguin Books, London

Dawkins, Richard (2006) *The God Delusion*, Bantam Press, a division of Transworld Publishers, London

Dennett, Daniel C. (1991) *Consciousness Explained*, Back Bay Books, Little, Brown and Company

Eysenck, Hans J. and Carl Sargent (1982) *Explaining the Unexplained: Mysteries of the Paranormal*, Book Club Associates

Goldacre, Ben (2009) *Bad Science*, Fourth Estate

Graves, Tom & Janet Hoult ed. (1982) *The Essential T. C. Lethbridge*, Granada Publishing Ltd

Harari, Yuval Noah (2011) *Sapiens: A Brief History of Humankind*, Vintage Books

Harari, Yuval Noah (2015) *Homo Deus: A Brief History of Tomorrow*, Harvill Secker

Hawking, Stephen (1988) *A Brief History of Time: From the Big Bang to Black Holes*, Guild Publishing London

Inglis, Brian (1994) *Science and Parascience: A History of the Paranormal, 1914-1939*, Hodder and Stoughton

Kaku, Michio (2008) *Physics of the Impossible: A Scientific Exploration of the World of Phasers, Force Fields, Teleportation and Time Travel*, Penguin Books

Kelly, Edward F. (2015) 'Parapsychology in Context: The Big Picture' in *Parapsychology: a handbook for the 21st century*, Jefferson, North Carolina: McFarland & Company, Inc., Publishers, Chapter 2, p.31

Kennedy, James E. (2000) 'Do People Guide Psi or Does Psi Guide People? Evidence and Implications from Life and Lab' *Journal of The American Society For Psychical Research*, 2000, 94:130-150

Kennedy, James E. (2014a) 'Experimenter Misconduct in Parapsychology: Analysis Manipulation and Fraud' http://jeksite.org/psi/misconduct.pdf

Kennedy, James E. (2016) Review of *Parapsychology: A Handbook for the 21st Century*, 2015, edited by Etzel Cardeña, John Palmer, and David Marcusson-Clavertz (This review is published on the internet in pdf and HTML at http://jeksite.org/psi/handbook_review.pdf and http://jeksite.org/psi/handbook_review.htm)

Koestler, Arthur (1974) *The Roots of Coincidence*, Picador

Lethbridge, T.C. (1965) *ESP: Beyond Time and Distance*, Sidgwick & Jackson, London

Meares, Ainslie (1969) *Strange Places and Simple Truths*, Souvenir Press

Nagel, Thomas (2012) *Mind and Cosmos: Why the Materialist Neo-Darwinian Conception of Nature is Almost Certainly False*, Oxford University Press

Picknett, Lynn (1987) *Flights of Fancy? 100 Years of Paranormal Experiences*, Ward Lock Limited, London

Powell, Dr Andrew (2017) *The Ways of the Soul – A Psychiatrist Reflects: Essays on Life, Death and Beyond*, Muswell Hill Press, London

Radin, Dean (1997) *The Conscious Universe: The Scientific Truth of Psychic Phenomena*, HarperEdge, Harper Collins

Radin, Dean (2006) *Entangled Minds: Extrasensory Experiences in a Quantum Reality*, Paraview Pocket Books

Richards, Steve (2015) *The Traveller's Guide to the Astral Plane*, Coronet, an imprint of Hodder & Stoughton, London

Rovelli, Carlo (2015) *Seven Brief Lessons on Physics*, Penguin Books

Schwartz, Gary E. R. and Linda G. S. Russek (1999) *The Living Energy Universe*, Hampton Roads

Schwartz, Gary E. with William L. Simon (1999?) *The Afterlife Experiments: Breakthrough Scientific Evidence of Life after Death*, Atrin Books, New York

Sheldrake, Rupert (1983) *A New Science of Life: The Hypothesis of Causative Formation*, Paladin Books

Sheldrake, Rupert (2004) *The Sense Of Being Stared At*, Arrow Books, Random House Group, London

Sheldrake, Rupert (2013) *The Science Delusion*, Coronet, an imprint of Hodder & Stoughton, London

Smith, Gordon (2016) *One Hundred Answers from Spirit: Britain's Greatest Medium Answers the Great Questions of Life and Death*, Coronet, an imprint of Hodder & Stoughton, London

Strawson, Galen (2018) *Things That Bother Me: Death, Freedom, the Self, Etc.*, The New York Review of Books

Sylvia, Claire (1998) *A Change of Heart*, Grand Central Publishing

Utts, Jessica (1999) *The Significance of Statistics in Mind-Matter Research*, http://citeseerx.ist.psu.edu/viewdoc/summary?doi=10.1.1.135.5667

Weinman, Ric (2013) *Awakening Through The Veils: A Seeker's Guide*, Balboa Press

Weinman, Ric A. (2015) *VortexHealing® Divine Energy Healing: A Magical Path of Healing and Awakening*, Balboa Press

Wilson, Colin ed. (1995) *The Giant Book of the Supernatural: Unlock the Earth's Hidden Mysteries*, Parragon

Zatta, Claudia (2017) *Interconnectedness. The Living World of the Early Greek Philosophers* https://www.academia.edu/34276448/Interconnectedness._The_Living_World_of_the_Early_Greek_Philosophers

Zukav, Gary (1980) *The Dancing Wu Li Masters: An Overview of the New Physics*, Fontana Paperbacks